ISBN 978-1-5400-9548-0

Visit Hal Leonard Online at
www.halleonard.com

Contact Us:
Hal Leonard
7777 West Bluemound Road
Milwaukee, WI 53213
Email: info@halleonard.com

In Europe, contact:
Hal Leonard Europe Limited
42 Wigmore Street
Marylebone, London, W1U 2RN
Email: info@halleonardeurope.com

In Australia, contact:
Hal Leonard Australia Pty. Ltd.
4 Lentara Court
Cheltenham, Victoria, 3192 Australia
Email: info@halleonard.com.au

The A Team

Words and Music by Ed Sheeran

____ team,   stuck in her ___ day - dream.   Been this way ___ since

eight - een, ___ but late - ly ____ her face seems ___ slow - ly sink - ing, wast -

- ing,   crum - bl - ing ___ like pas - tries.   And they ___ scream: The worst ___

____ things   in ____ life come free   to   us, _____ { (1., 2.) 'cause   we're
                                                          { (D.S.)   and   we're

Chorus

just   un - der the up - per hand ___   and go mad for a cou - ple grams. _
all   un - der the up - per hand ___   and go mad for a cou - ple grams. _

And she don't wan - na go _____ out - side _____ to - night. _   And in a
And we don't wan - na go _____ out - side _____ to - night. _   And in a

night   straight down the line.   (Ooh. _____

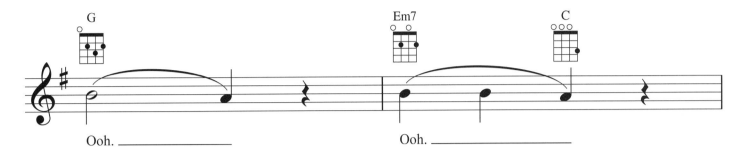

Ooh. _____   Ooh. _____

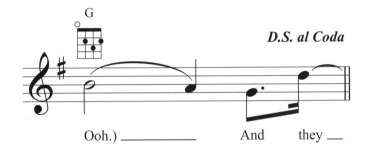

D.S. al Coda

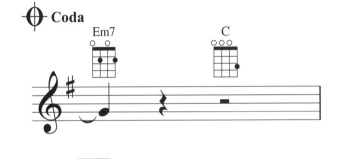

⊕ Coda

Ooh.) _____   And   they _____   _____

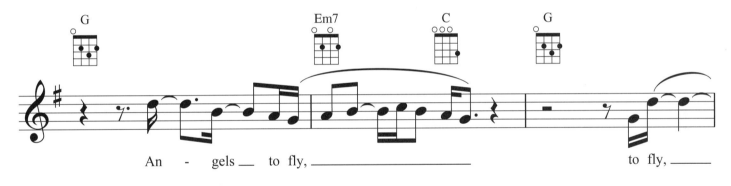

An - gels ___ to fly, _____   to fly, _____

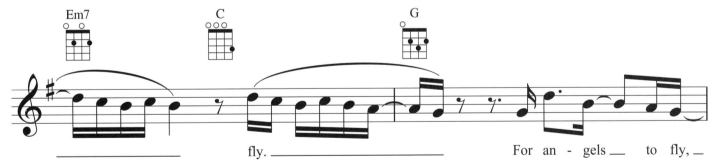

_____ to fly, _____   fly. _____   For an - gels ___ to fly, _____

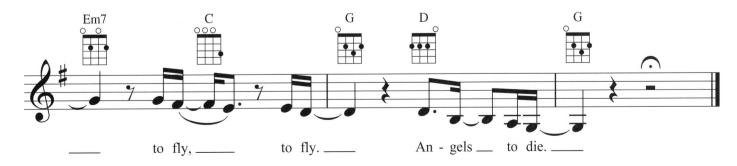

_____ to fly, _____   to fly. _____   An - gels ___ to die. _____

American Pie

Words and Music by Don McLean

First note

A long, long time a-go ___ I can still re-mem - ber how that

mu - sic used to make me smile. ___ And I knew if I had my chance that

I could make _ those peo-ple dance _ and may-be they'd _ be hap-py ___ for a

while. But Feb-ru-ar-y made me shiv-er,

with ev - 'ry pa - per I'd de - liv - er. Bad news on the door - step, I

could - n't take one more step. I can't re - mem - ber if I cried ____ when I

read a - bout ___ his wid - owed bride. ___ Some - thing touched me deep in - side, ____ the

day the mu - sic died. So,

Chorus
Moderately ♩ = 102

bye, ____ bye, Miss A - mer - i - can Pie. ___ Drove ___ my Chev - y to the lev - ee, but the

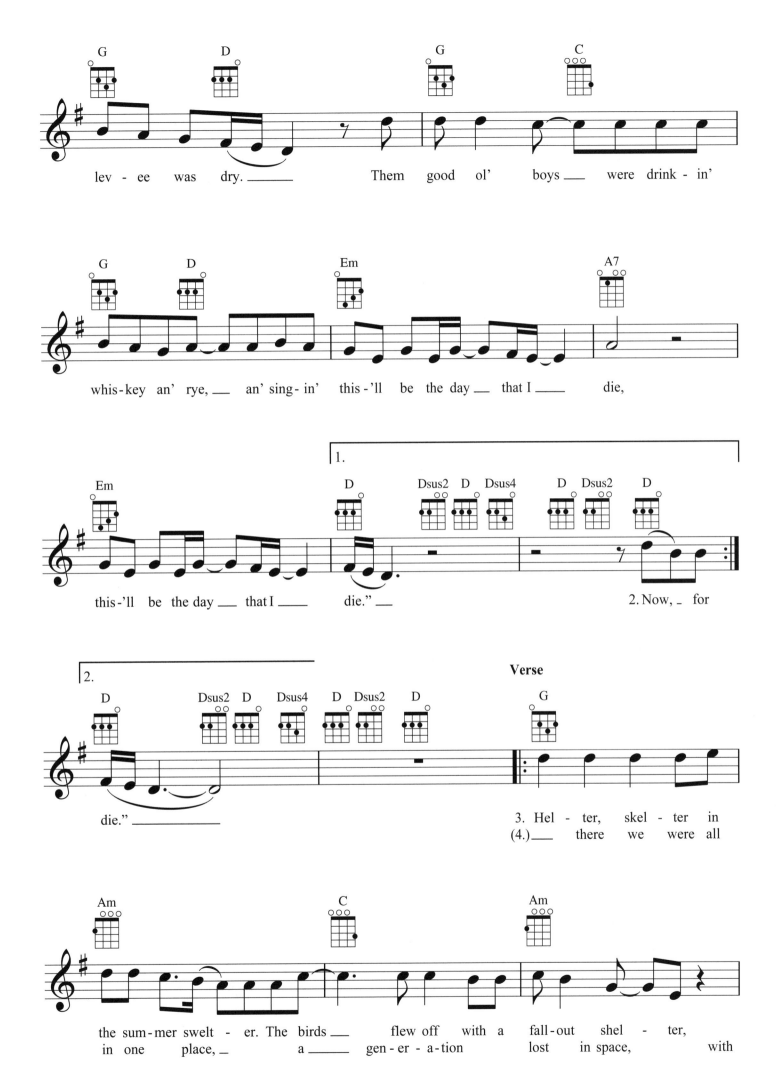

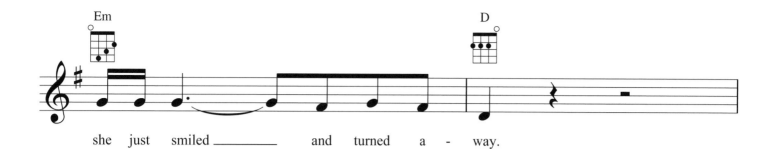

she just smiled _____ and turned a - way.

I went down to the sa - cred store _ where I'd heard the mu - sic years be - fore. __ But the

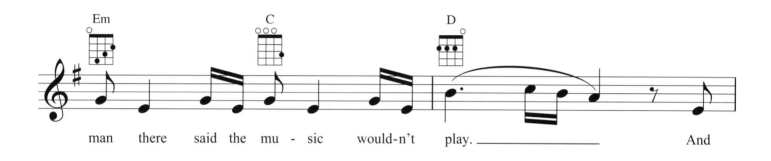

man there said the mu - sic would-n't play. _____ And

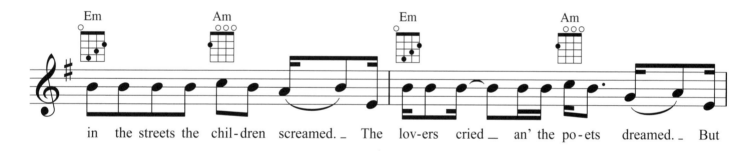

in the streets the chil-dren screamed. _ The lov-ers cried _ an' the po - ets dreamed. _ But

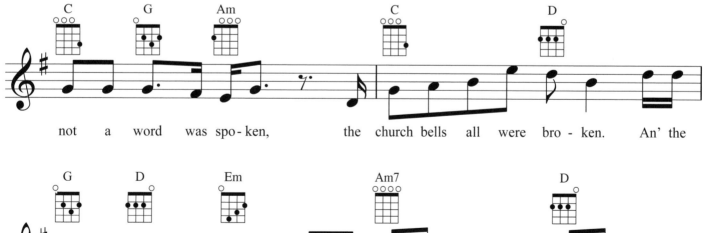

not a word was spo - ken, the church bells all were bro - ken. An' the

three men I ad - mire _ most, ___ the Fa - ther, Son and _ the Ho - ly Ghost, they

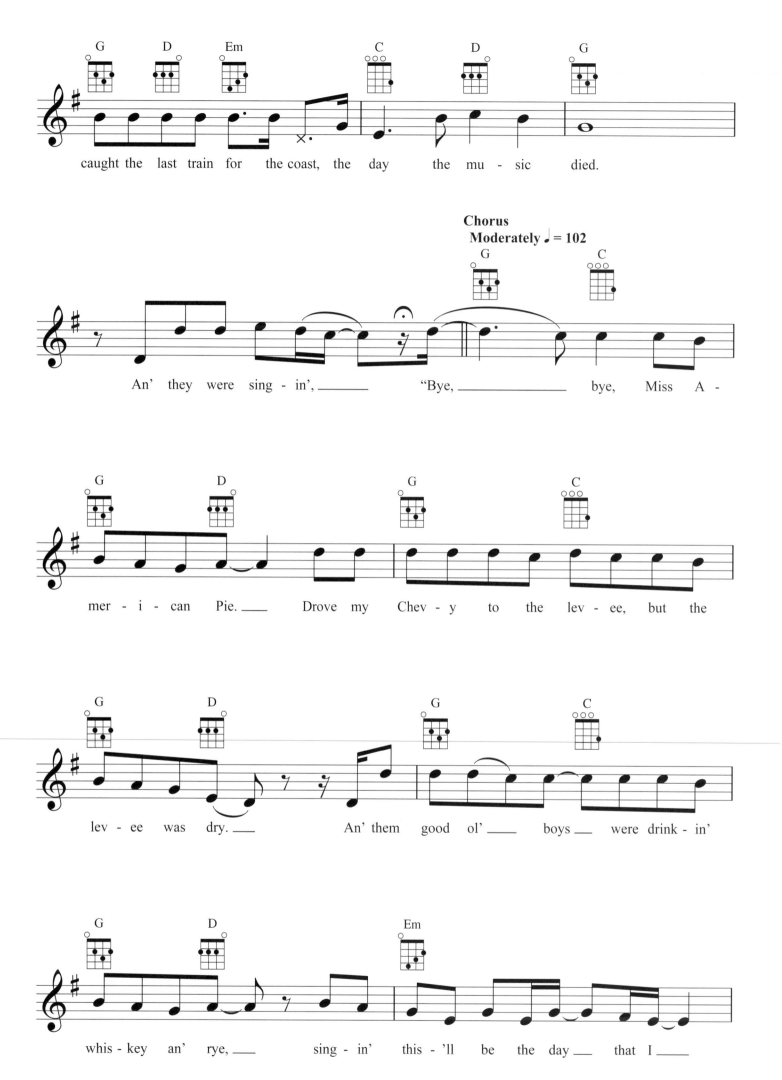

caught the last train for the coast, the day the mu - sic died.

Chorus
Moderately ♩ = 102

An' they were sing - in', _____ "Bye, _____ bye, Miss A -

mer - i - can Pie. ___ Drove my Chev - y to the lev - ee, but the

lev - ee was dry. ___ An' them good ol' ___ boys ___ were drink - in'

whis - key an' rye, ___ sing - in' this - 'll be the day ___ that I _____

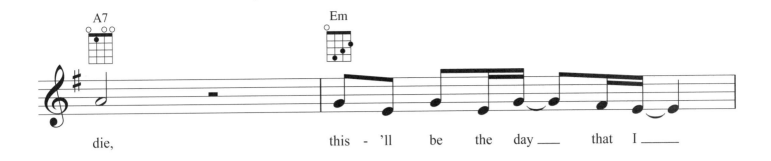

die,   this - 'll be the day ___ that I ___

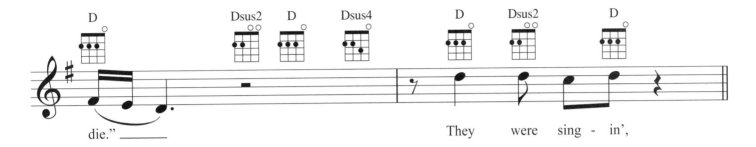

die." ___   They were sing - in',

Outro-Chorus

"Bye, ___ bye, Miss A - mer - i - can Pie. ___   Drove my

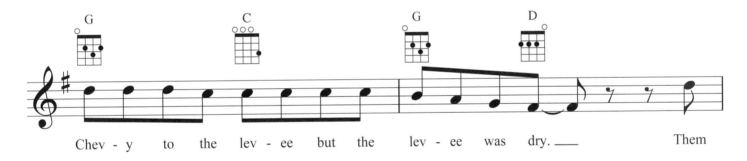

Chev - y to the lev - ee but the lev - ee was dry. ___   Them

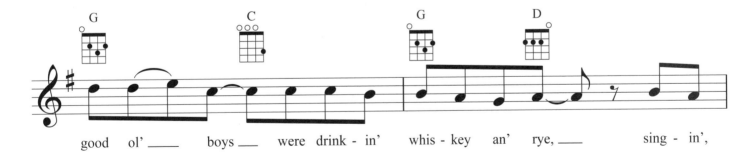

good ol' ___ boys ___ were drink - in' whis - key an' rye, ___   sing - in',

this - 'll be the day ___ that I ___ die." ___

Baby, I Love Your Way

Words and Music by Peter Frampton

Pre-Chorus

don't   hes - i - tate ____   'cause your

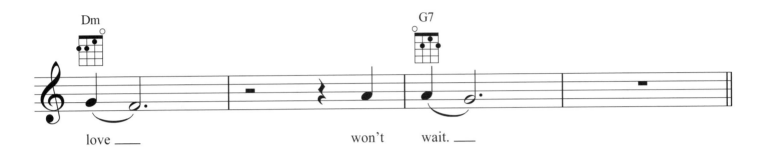

love ____   won't   wait. ____

Chorus

Ooh,   ba - by, I love ___ your way. ____

Wan - na   tell you I love ___ your way. ____

Wan - na   be with you night ___ and day. ____

Interlude

To Coda

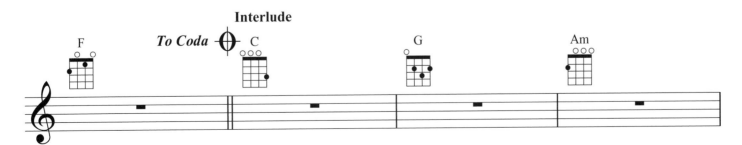

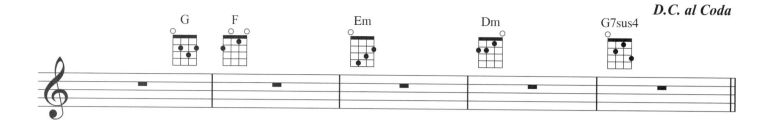

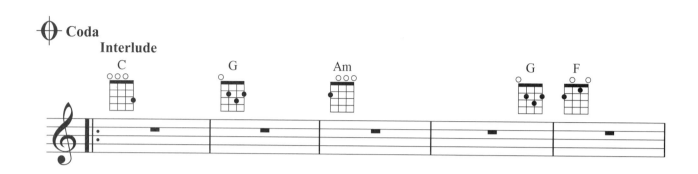

Coda
Interlude

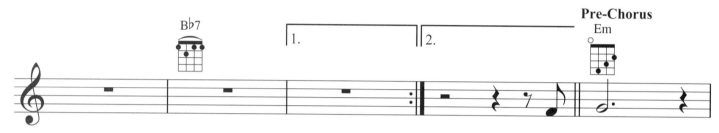

But   don't

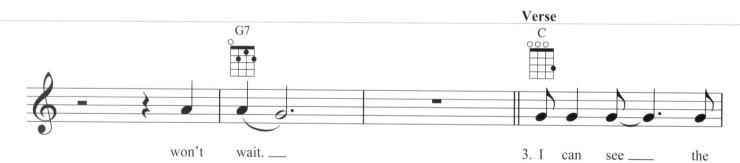

hes - i - tate ____   'cause your   love ____

Verse

won't   wait. ____   3. I   can   see ____   the

sun - set   in your   eyes, ____   brown and   gray

Bad Moon Rising

Words and Music by John Fogerty

Additional Lyrics

2. I hear hurricanes a-blowin'.
   I know the end is comin' soon.
   I fear rivers overflowin'.
   I hear the voice of rage and ruin.

3. Hope you got your things together.
   Hope you are quite prepared to die.
   Looks like we're in for nasty weather.
   One eye is taken for an eye.

Better Together

Words and Music by Jack Johnson

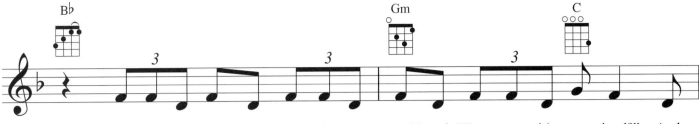

"Why are we here?" and "Where do we go?" and "How come it's so hard?" And

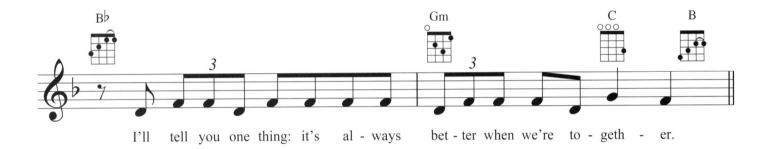

it's not al-ways eas-y and some-times life can be de-ceiv - ing.

I'll tell you one thing: it's al-ways bet-ter when we're to-geth - er.

Chorus

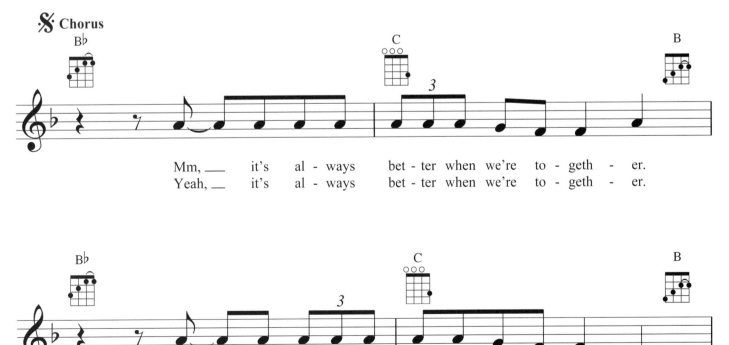

Mm, ___ it's al-ways bet-ter when we're to-geth - er.
Yeah, ___ it's al-ways bet-ter when we're to-geth - er.

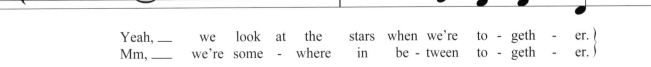

Yeah, ___ we look at the stars when we're to-geth - er.
Mm, ___ we're some-where in be-tween to-geth - er.

Well, __ it's al-ways bet-ter when we're to-geth - er.

Yeah, __ it's al-ways bet-ter when we're to-geth - er. _____

2. And all of these

mo-ments just might find a way in-to my dreams __ to-night, __ but I

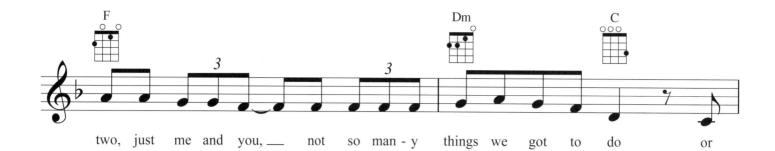

two, just me and you, ___ not so man - y things we got to do or

D.S. al Coda

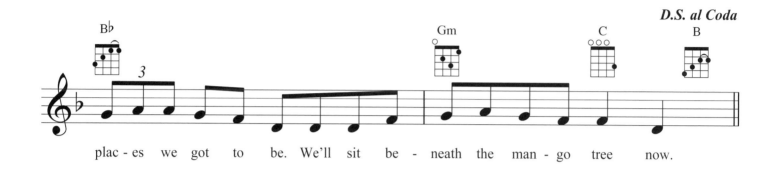

plac - es we got to be. We'll sit be - neath the man - go tree now.

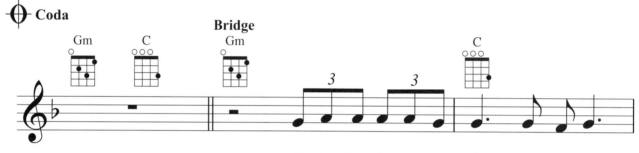

Coda   Bridge

I be - lieve in mem - o - ries; they look so,

so pret - ty when I sleep. ___ Hey, now and, ___ and when I wake ___

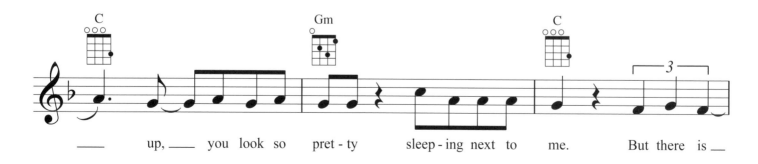

___ up, ___ you look so pret - ty sleep - ing next to me. But there is ___

not e - nough time. _____ And there is no, ___

___ no song I could sing. _____ And there is no ___

___ com - bi - na - tion of words ___ I could say, ___ but I will

Outro

still tell you one thing: ___ We're bet - ter to - geth - er. _____

Building a Mystery

Words and Music by Sarah McLachlan and Pierre Marchand

Cat's in the Cradle

Words and Music by Harry Chapin and Sandy Chapin

First note

Verse
Moderate Folk style, in 2

1. My child ar - rived __ just the oth - er day; he
(2., 3.) *See additional lyrics*

came to the world in the u - su - al way. __ But there were planes to catch __ and

bills to pay; __ he learned to walk while I was a - way. And he was

talk - in' 'fore I knew it, and as he grew he'd say, "I'm gon - na be like

Outro-Chorus

Additional Lyrics

2. My son turned ten just the other day;
   He said, "Thanks for the ball, Dad. Come on, let's play.
   Can you teach me to throw?"
   I said, "Not today, I got a lot to do."
   He said, "That's okay." And he, he walked away,
   But his smile never dimmed, it said,
   "I'm gonna be like him, yeah.
   You know I'm gonna be like him."

3. Well, he came from college just the other day;
   So much like a man I just had to say,
   "Son, I'm proud of you. Can you sit for a while?"
   He shook his head and he said with a smile,
   "What I'd really like, Dad, is to borrow the car keys.
   See you later; can I have them, please?"

Chasing Cars

Words and Music by Gary Lightbody, Tom Simpson, Paul Wilson, Jonathan Quinn and Nathan Connolly

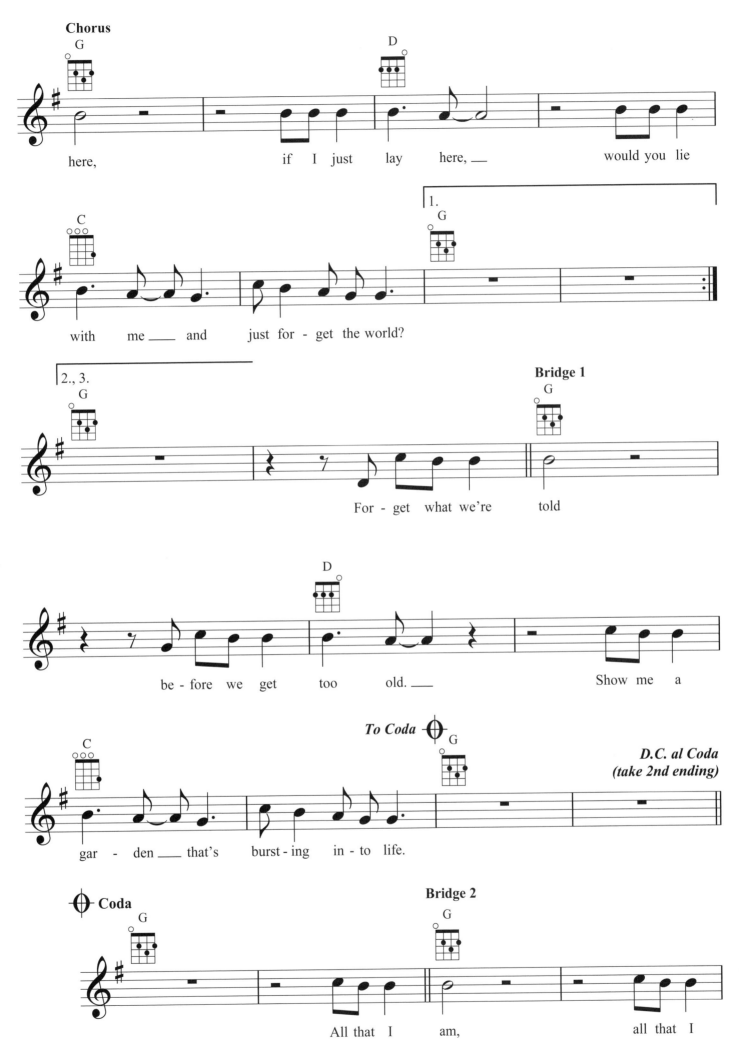

ev - er was __   is here in your per - fect __ eyes,

they're all I can see.   I don't know where,

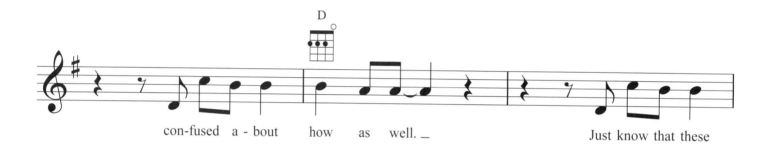

con - fused a - bout how as well. __   Just know that these

things will nev - er change __ for us at all.   If I lay

Outro-Chorus

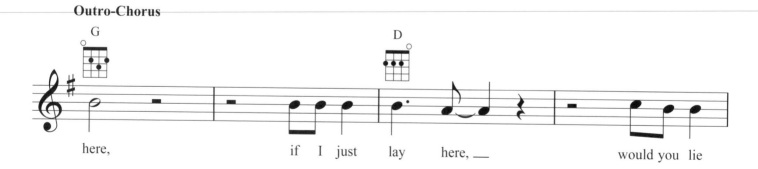

here,   if I just lay here, __   would you lie

with me __ and just for - get the world?

Brown Eyed Girl

Words and Music by Van Morrison

in the mist - y morn - ing fog __ with our

hearts a - thump - in', and you, _____ my brown eyed girl. __

__ You, _____

1.

_____ my brown eyed girl. _____

2., 3.

Do you re - mem - ber when __ we used to sing: __

Chorus

_____ Sha, la, __ la, la, _____ la, la, __ la, la, __ la, la, la, te, da? __

Sha, la, ___ la, la, ___ la, la, ___ la, la, ___ la, la, la, te, da.

Coda   **Outro-Chorus**

We used to sing: Sha, la, ___ la, la, ___

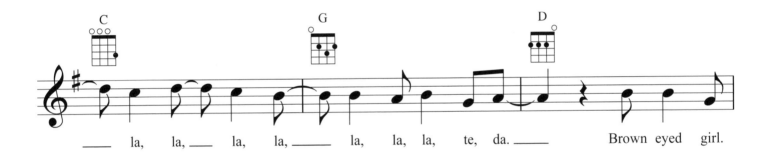

___ la, la, ___ la, la, ___ la, la, la, te, da. ___ Brown eyed girl.

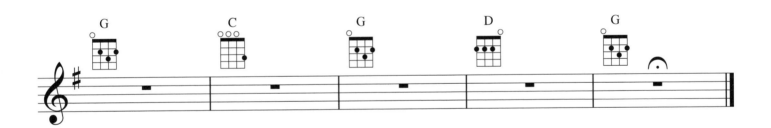

Additional Lyrics

2. Whatever happened
   To Tuesday and so slow?
   Going down the old mine.
   With a transistor radio.
   Standing in the sunlight laughing,
   Hiding behind a rainbow's wall,
   Slipping and sliding
   All along the waterfall with you,
   My brown eyed girl.
   You, my brown eyed girl.

3. So hard to find my way
   Now that I'm all on my own.
   I saw you just the other day;
   My, how you have grown.
   Cast my mem'ry back there, Lord.
   Sometimes I'm overcome thinking 'bout it.
   Laughing and a running, hey, hey.
   Behind the stadium with you.
   My brown eyed girl.
   A you, my brown eyed girl.

Count on Me

Words and Music by Bruno Mars, Ari Levine and Philip Lawrence

1. If you ev-er find your-self stuck in the mid-dle of the sea, _____
(2.) *See additional lyrics*

I'll sail _____ the world _____

to find _____ you. If you

ev-er find your-self lost in the dark, and you can't see, _____

I'll be _____ the light _____ to guide _____

Pre-Chorus

_____ you. We

find out what ___ we're made of when we ___

_____ are called _ to help ___ our friends _ in need.

𝄋 Chorus

You can count on me like

"one, two, three." I'll be _____ there.

And I know when I need it, I can

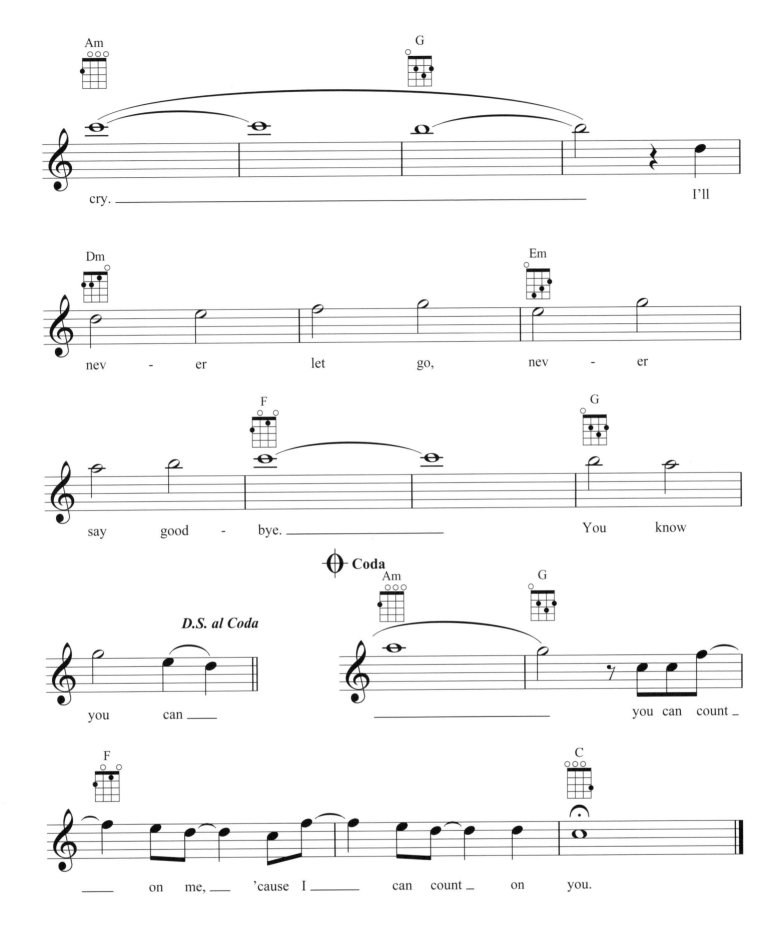

Additional Lyrics

2. If you're tossin' and you're turnin'
   And you just can't fall asleep,
   I'll sing a song beside you.
   And if you ever forget how much
   You really mean to me,
   Ev'ry day I will remind you.

Good Riddance
(Time of Your Life)

Words by Billie Joe
Music by Green Day

Hey Jude

Words and Music by John Lennon and Paul McCartney

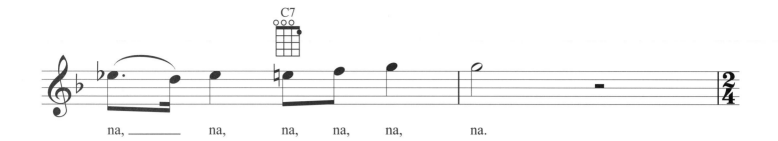

na, _____ na, na, na, na, na.

Verse

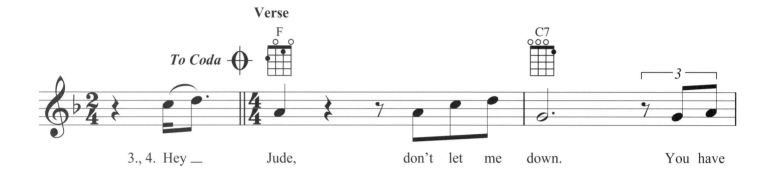

3., 4. Hey _ Jude, don't let me down. You have

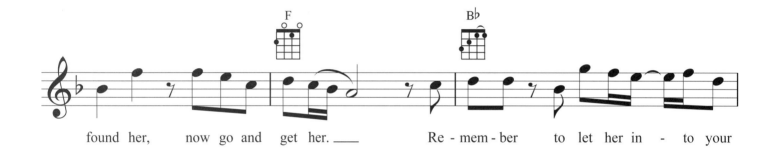

found her, now go and get her. ___ Re - mem - ber to let her in - to your

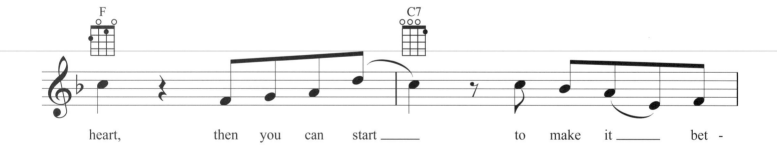

heart, then you can start _____ to make it _____ bet -

D.S. al Coda

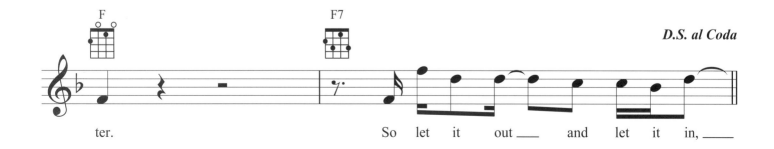

ter. So let it out ___ and let it in, ___

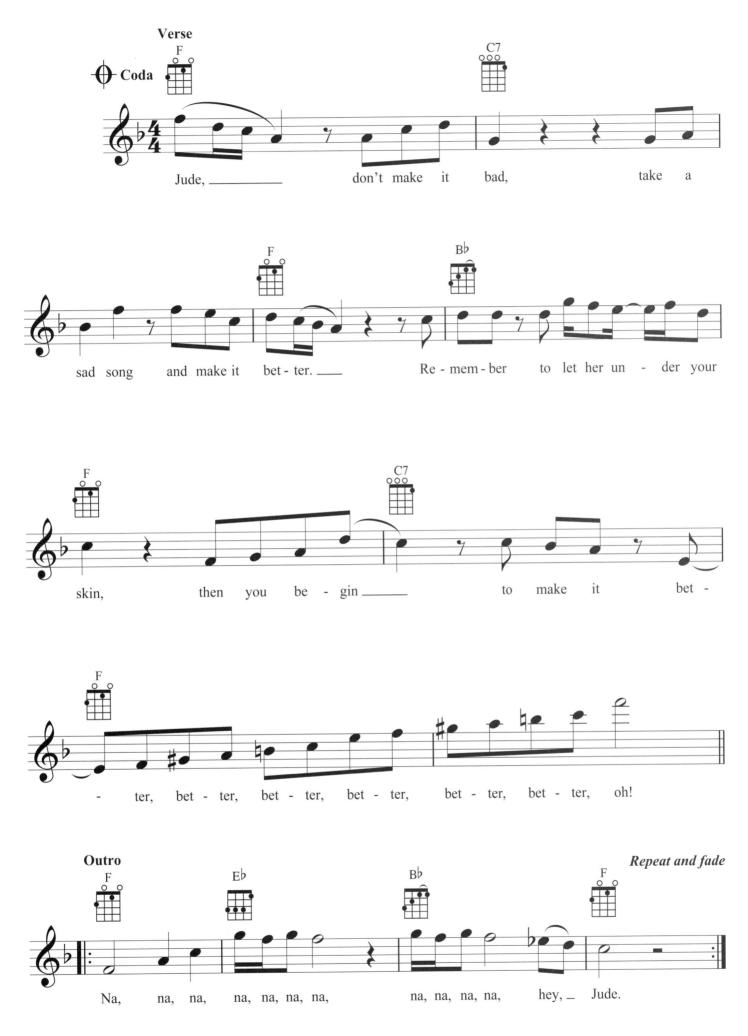

Hey There Delilah

Words and Music by Tom Higgenson

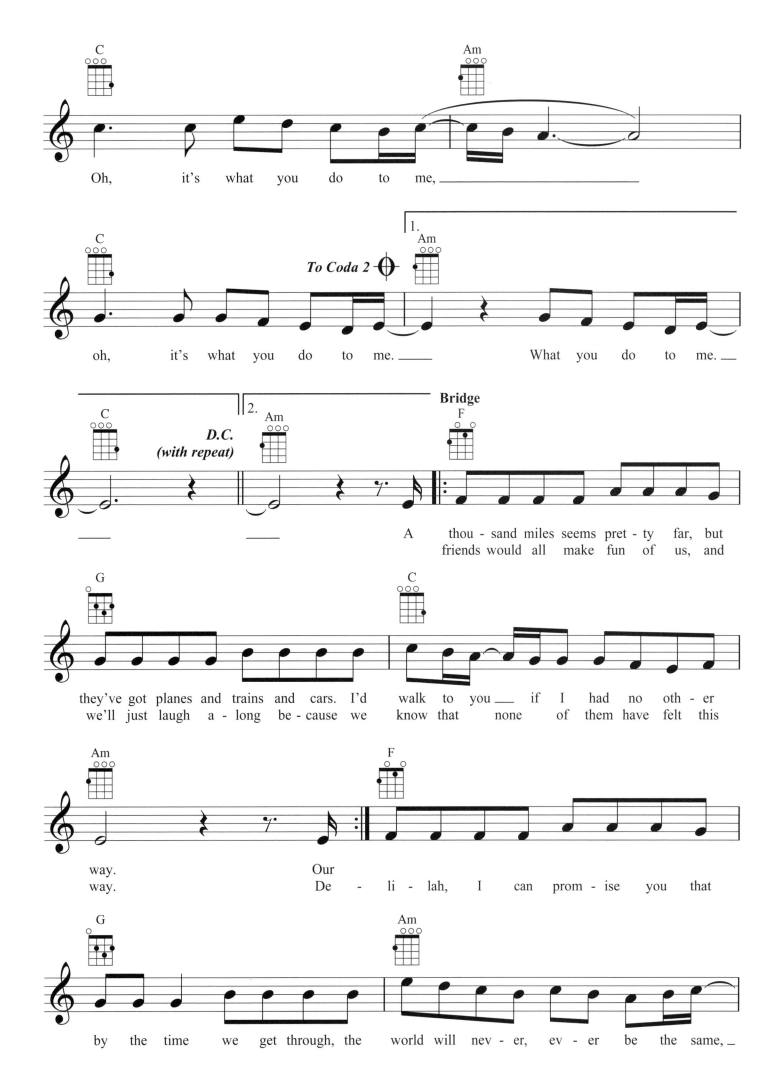

Oh, it's what you do to me, _____

oh, it's what you do to me. _____ What you do to me. __

_____   _____   A thou - sand miles seems pret - ty far, but
                          friends would all make fun of us, and

they've got planes and trains and cars. I'd walk to you __ if I had no oth - er
we'll just laugh a - long be - cause we know that none of them have felt this

way.   Our
way.   De - li - lah, I can prom - ise you that

by the time we get through, the world will nev - er, ev - er be the same, __

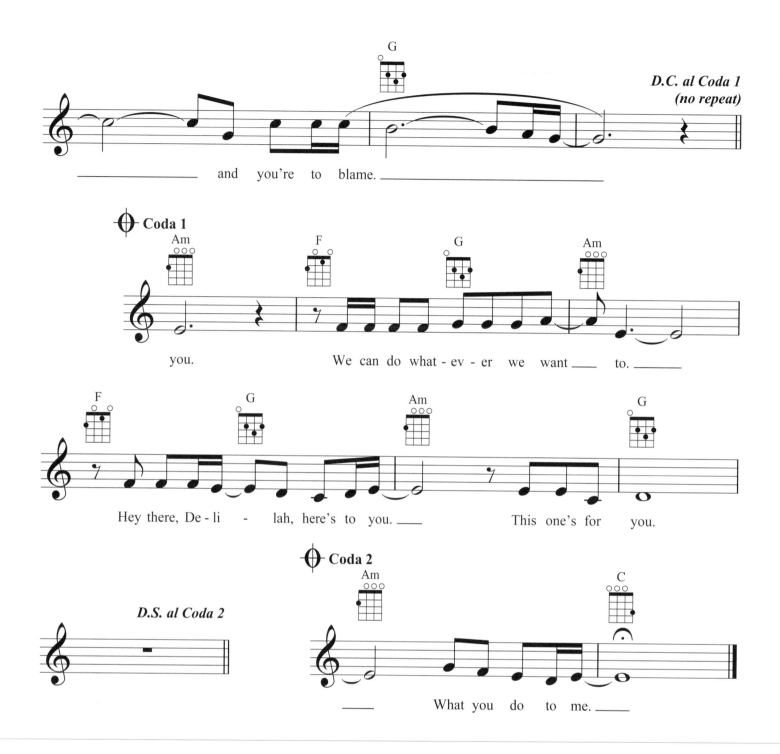

D.C. al Coda 1
(no repeat)

and you're to blame.

Coda 1

you.   We can do what - ev - er we want ___ to. ___

Hey there, De - li - lah, here's to you. ___   This one's for   you.

D.S. al Coda 2

Coda 2

___   What you do to me. ___

Additional Lyrics

2. Hey there, Delilah, don't you worry about the distance.
   I'm right there if you get lonely; give this song another listen, close your eyes.
   Listen to my voice; it's my disguise. I'm by your side.

3. Hey there, Delilah, I know times are getting hard,
   But just believe me, girl, someday I'll pay the bills with this guitar. We'll have it good.
   We'll have the life we knew we would. My word is good.

4. Hey there, Delilah, I've got so much left to say.
   If ev'ry simple song I wrote to you would take your breath away, I'd write it all.
   Even more in love with me you'd fall. We'd have it all.

5. Hey there, Delilah, you be good and don't you miss me.
   Two more years and you'll be done with school, and I'll be making hist'ry like I do.
   You'll know it's all because of you. *(To Coda 1)*

Daughter

Words by Eddie Vedder
Music by Eddie Vedder, Stone Gossard, Jeff Ament, Mike McCready and Dave Abbruzzese

tries to un-der-stand ___ it, tries to make ___ her proud.

Pre-Chorus

The shades ___ go down. It's in ___ her ___ head, ___

___ paint - ed ___ room, ___ can't ___ de - ny ___

𝄋 Chorus

___ there's some - thing wrong. ___ Don't call ___ me ___ daugh - ter, ___

___ not fit ___ to. The pic - ture kept ___

___ will re - mind ___ me. Don't call ___ me ___ daugh - ter, ___

58

Home

Words and Music by Greg Holden and Drew Pearson

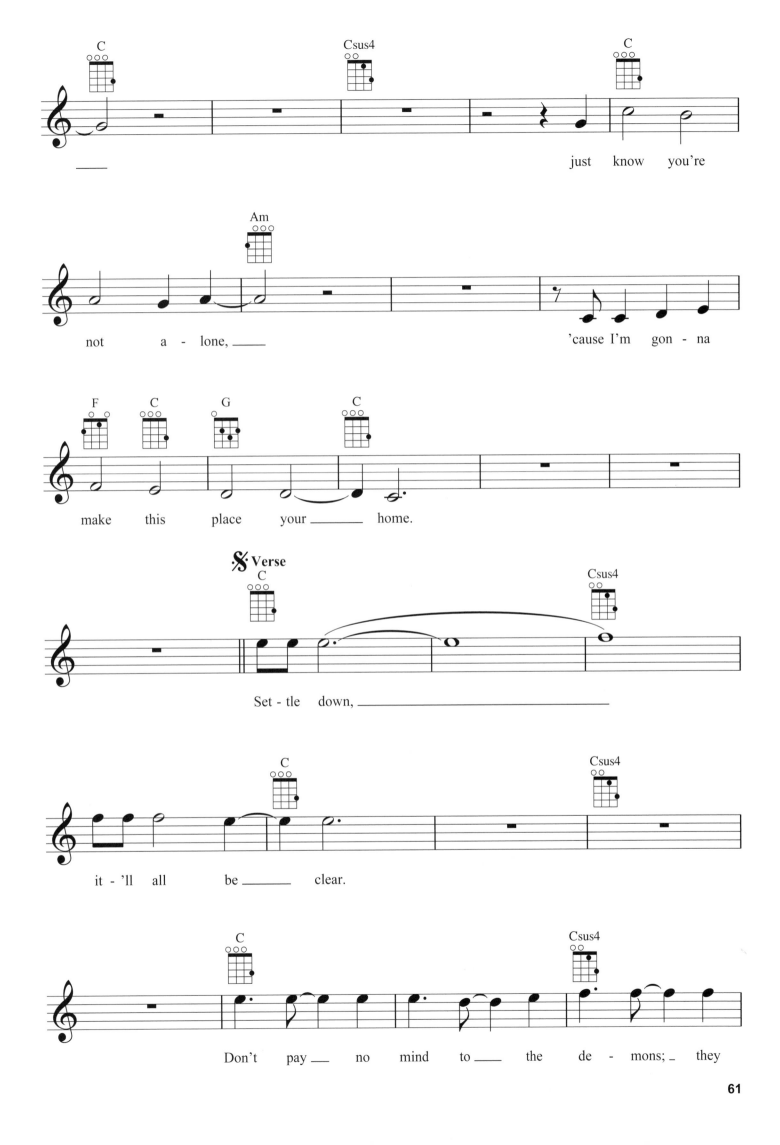

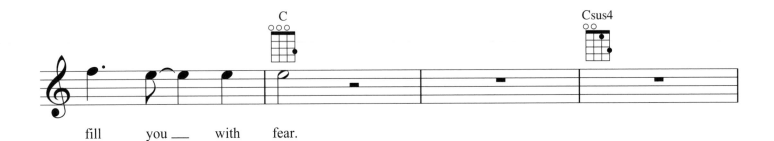

fill you __ with fear.

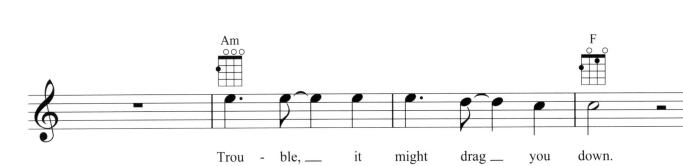

Trou - ble, __ it might drag __ you down.

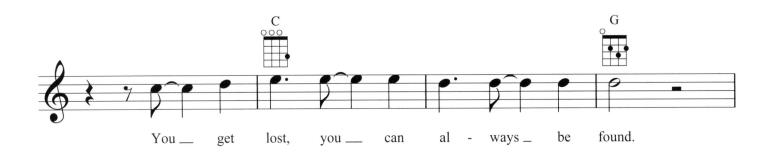

You __ get lost, you __ can al - ways __ be found.

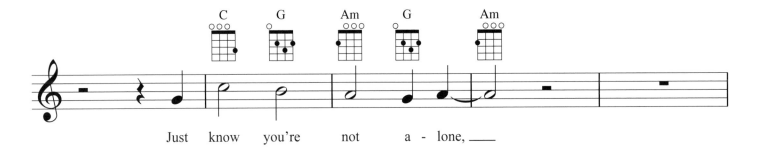

Just know you're not a - lone, ___

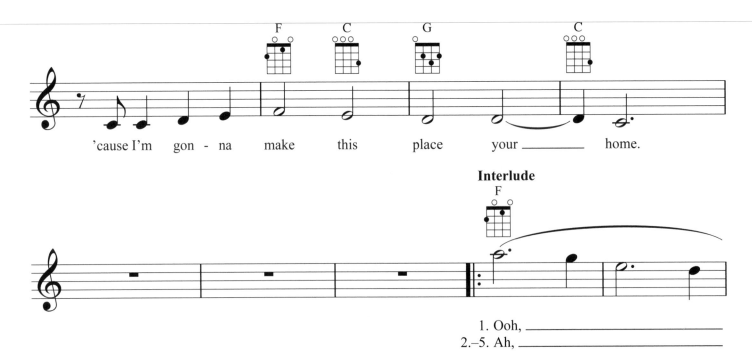

'cause I'm gon - na make this place your _____ home.

Interlude

1. Ooh, _____
2.–5. Ah, _____

ooh.

ah.

Ooh.

Ah.

1., 2., 4.

3. **D.S.** **5.** **Outro**

Ah,

ah.

Ah.

House of Gold

Words and Music by Tyler Joseph

* To match recording, strum single string (xxx3) for the first 8 bars (first time only).

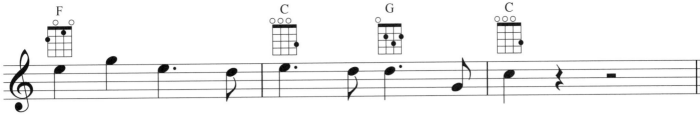

turns to stone, will you take care of me?"

Chorus

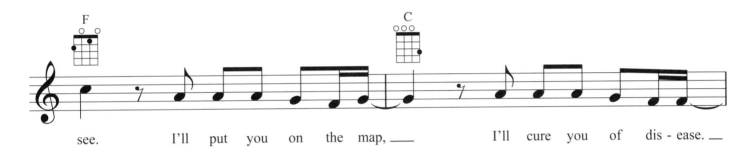

I will make you queen ____ of ev - 'ry - thing you

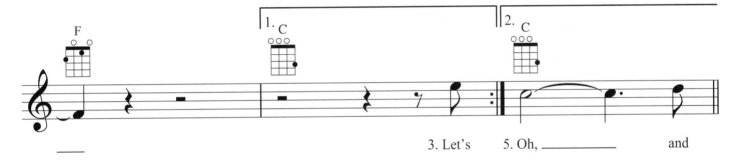

see. I'll put you on the map, ___ I'll cure you of dis - ease. ___

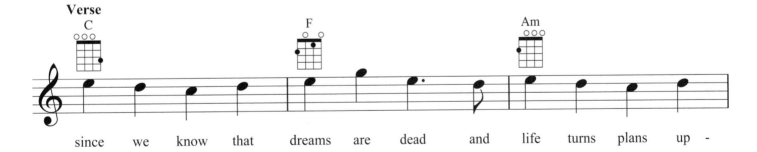

___ 3. Let's 5. Oh, _____ and

Verse

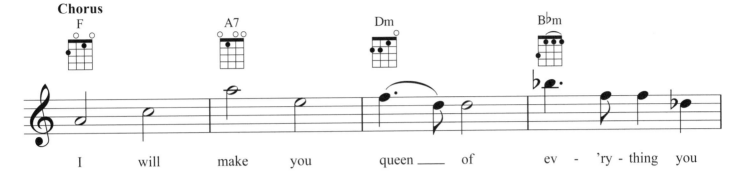

since we know that dreams are dead and life turns plans up -

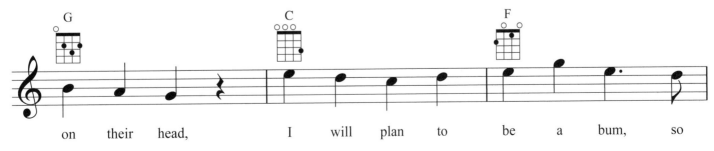

on their head, I will plan to be a bum, so

Hey Ya!

Words and Music by Andre Benjamin

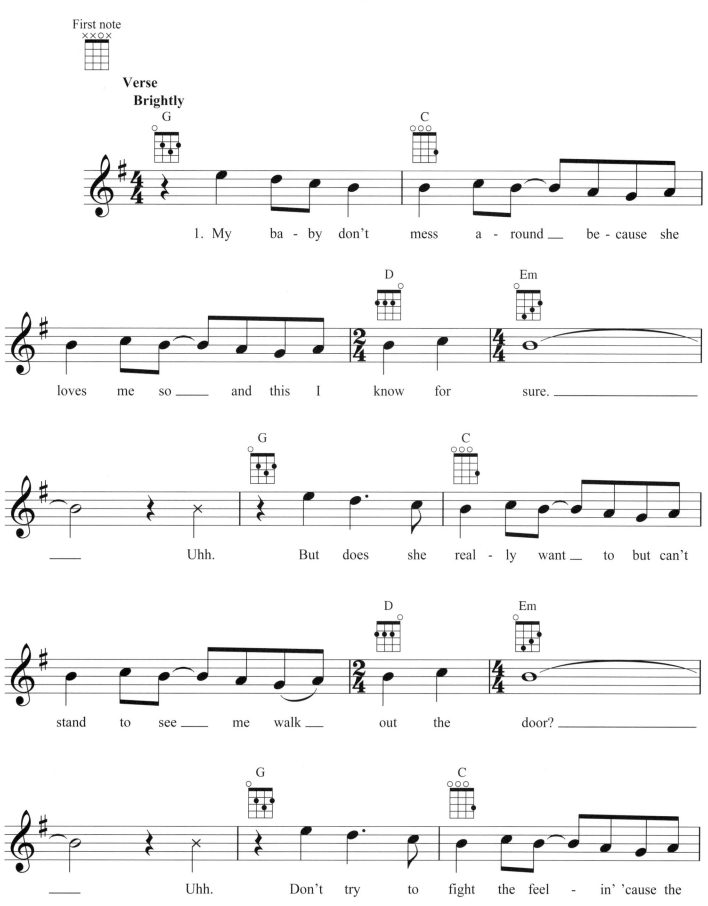

thought a - lone ___ is kill - ing me right now. _____

___ Uhh. Thank God for mom and dad ___ for stick - ing

two to - geth - er 'cause we don't know how. _____

Chorus

___ Uhh. Hey _____ ya! _____

Play 4 times

___ Hey _____ ya! _____

Verse

2. You think you've got it. Oh, ___ you think you've got it. But

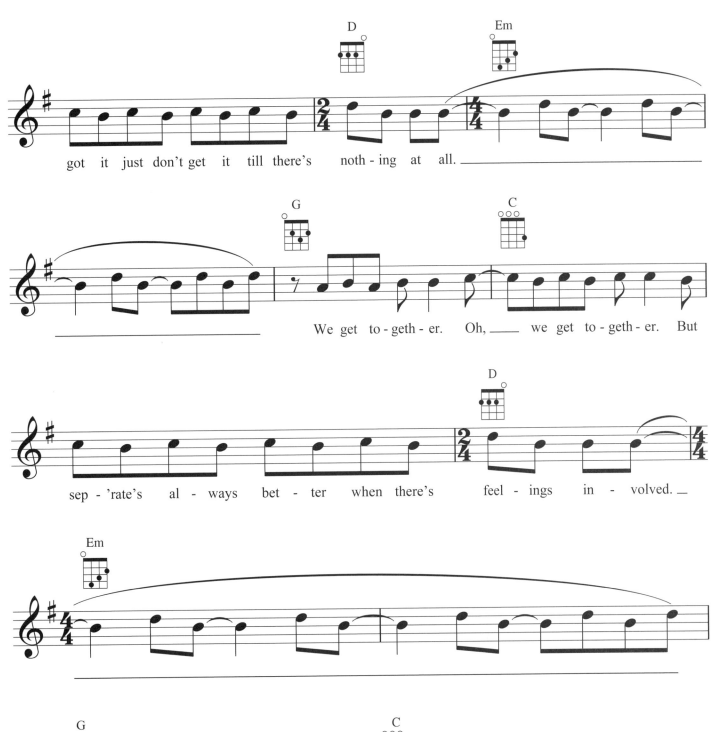

got it just don't get it till there's noth - ing at all. _____

We get to - geth - er. Oh, ____ we get to - geth - er. But

sep - 'rate's al - ways bet - ter when there's feel - ings in - volved. __

If what they say is, "Noth - ing is for - ev - er," then

what makes, then what makes, then what makes, then

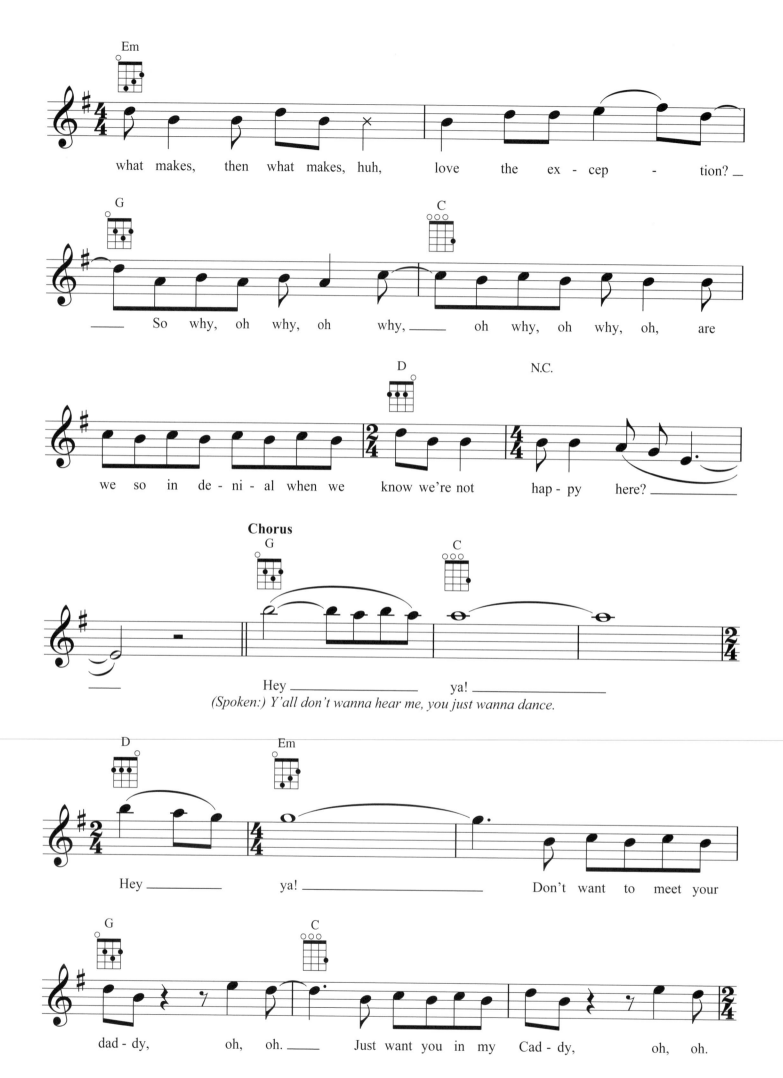

what makes, then what makes, huh, love the ex - cep - tion? So why, oh why, oh why, oh why, oh why, oh, are we so in de - ni - al when we know we're not hap - py here?

Chorus

Hey ya!

(Spoken:) Y'all don't wanna hear me, you just wanna dance.

Hey ya! Don't want to meet your dad - dy, oh, oh. Just want you in my Cad - dy, oh, oh.

Oh, oh, _____ don't want to meet your

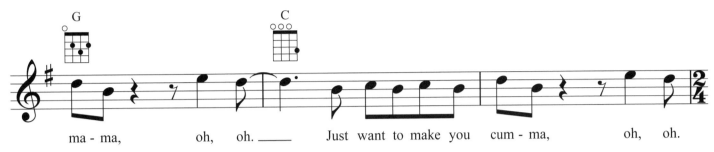

ma - ma, oh, oh. _____ Just want to make you cum - ma, oh, oh.

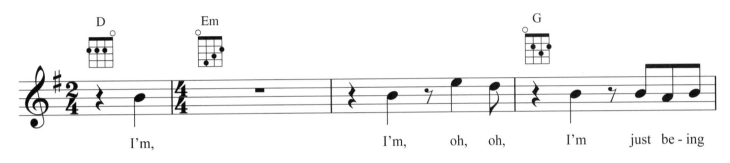

I'm, I'm, oh, oh, I'm just be - ing

hon - est. Oh, oh, _____ I'm just be - ing hon - est.

Outro-Chorus

Hey _____ ya! _____

Repeat and fade

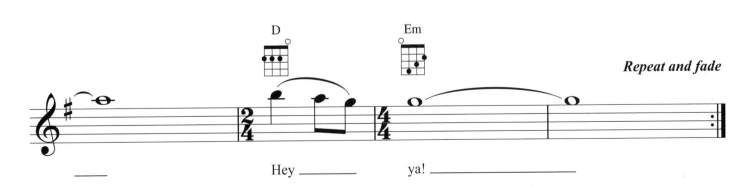

Hey _____ ya! _____

How to Save a Life

Words and Music by Joseph King and Isaac Slade

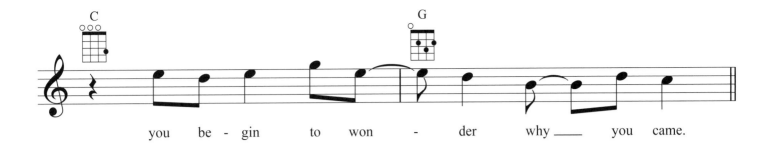

you be - gin to won - der why ____ you came.

Chorus

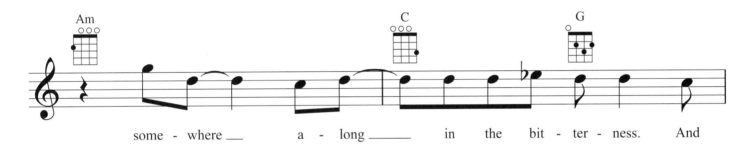

Where did I ____ go wrong? ____ } I lost _____ a friend

where did I ____ go wrong? ____ }

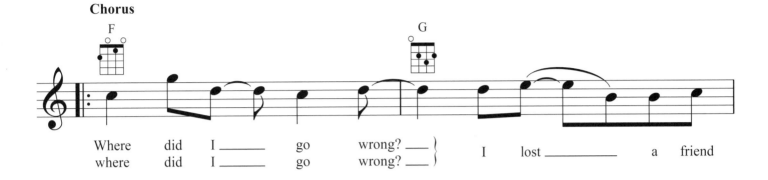

some - where ____ a - long _____ in the bit - ter - ness. And

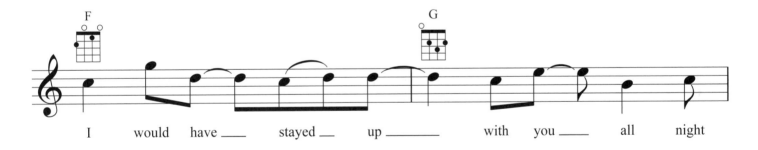

I would have ____ stayed ___ up _____ with you ____ all night

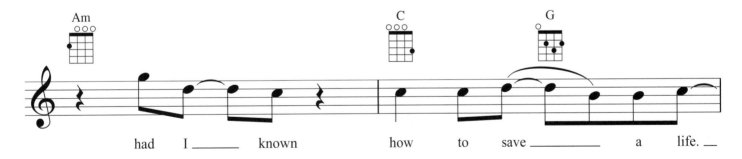

had I ____ known how to save _____ a life. __

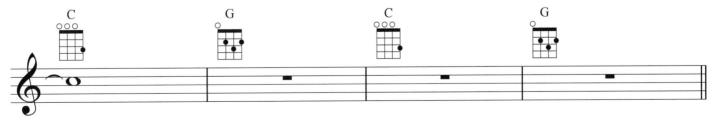

____

3. As

Verse

I Can See Clearly Now

Words and Music by Johnny Nash

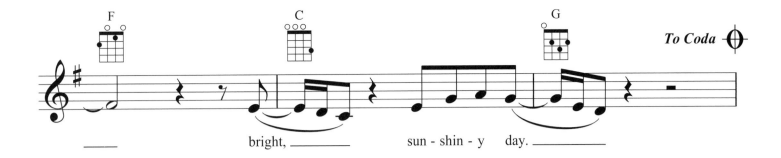

bright, sun-shin-y day._

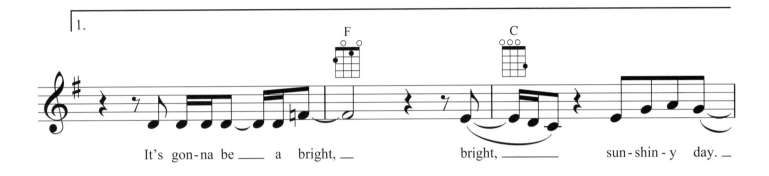

1.

It's gon-na be __ a bright, __ bright, _____ sun-shin-y day. __

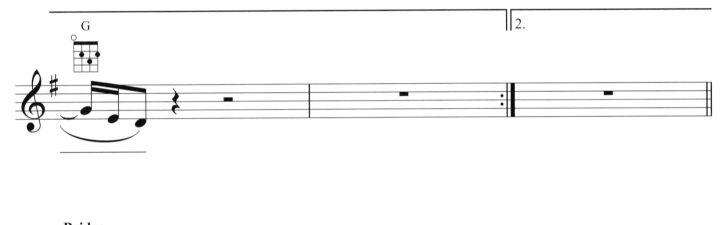

2.

Bridge

Look all a-round, _____ there's noth-ing but blue skies. _____

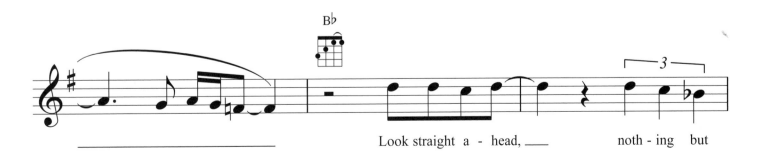

Look straight a-head, __ noth-ing but

To Coda ⊕

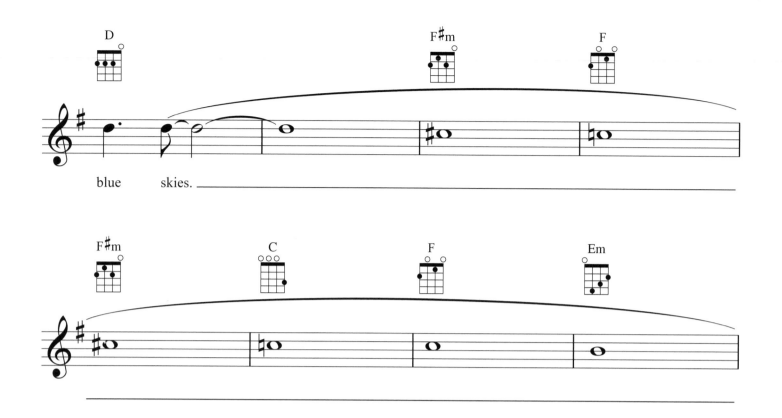

blue   skies. _____

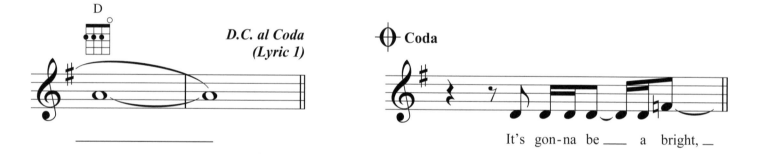

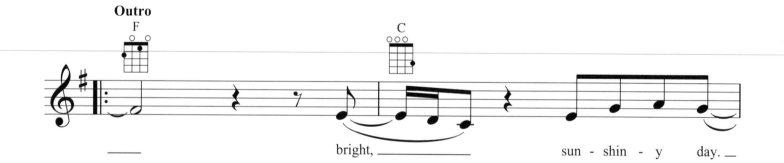

D.C. al Coda
(Lyric 1)

_____

Coda

It's gon-na be ___ a bright, ___

Outro

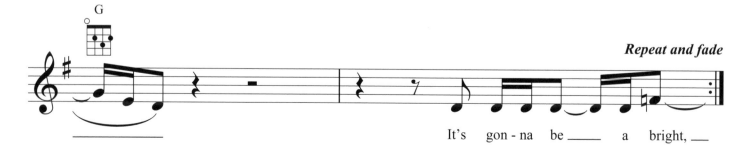

___   bright, _____   sun - shin - y   day. ___

Repeat and fade

It's   gon-na   be ___ a   bright, ___

78

Hurt

Words and Music by Trent Reznor

I will make __ you hurt. __

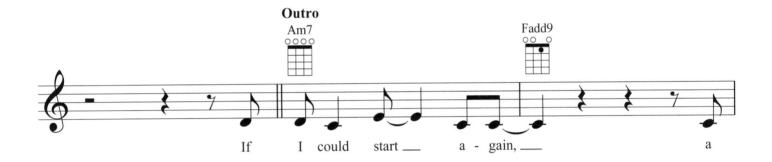

I will make __ you hurt.

Outro

If I could start __ a - gain, __ a

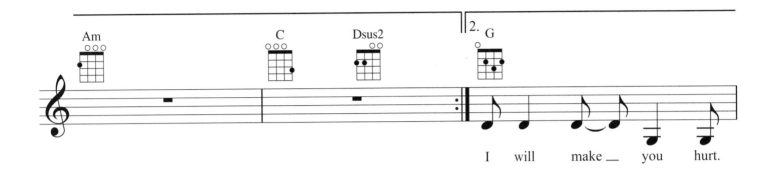

mil - lion miles __ a - way, __ I would keep __ my - self, __

__ I would find __ a way.

I Will Follow You into the Dark

Words and Music by Benjamin Gibbard

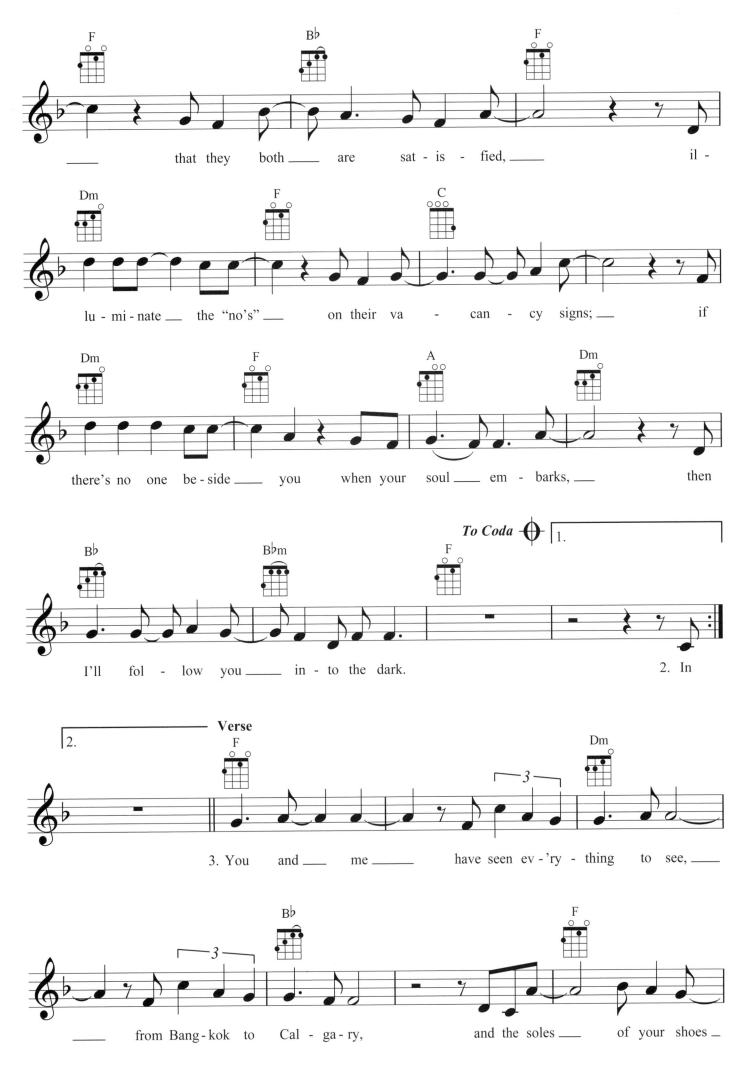

that they both ___ are sat - is - fied, _____ il -

lu - mi - nate ___ the "no's" ___ on their va - can - cy signs; ___ if

there's no one be - side ___ you when your soul ___ em - barks, ___ then

To Coda ⊕ | 1.

I'll fol - low you _____ in - to the dark. 2. In

Verse

| 2.

3. You and ___ me ___ have seen ev - 'ry - thing to see, ___

from Bang - kok to Cal - ga - ry, and the soles ___ of your shoes ___

D.S. al Coda

Additional Lyrics

2. In Catholic school, as vicious as Roman rule,
   I got my knuckles bruised by a lady in black.
   I held my tongue as she told me, "Son,
   Fear is the heart of love." So I never went back.

Island in the Sun

Words and Music by Rivers Cuomo

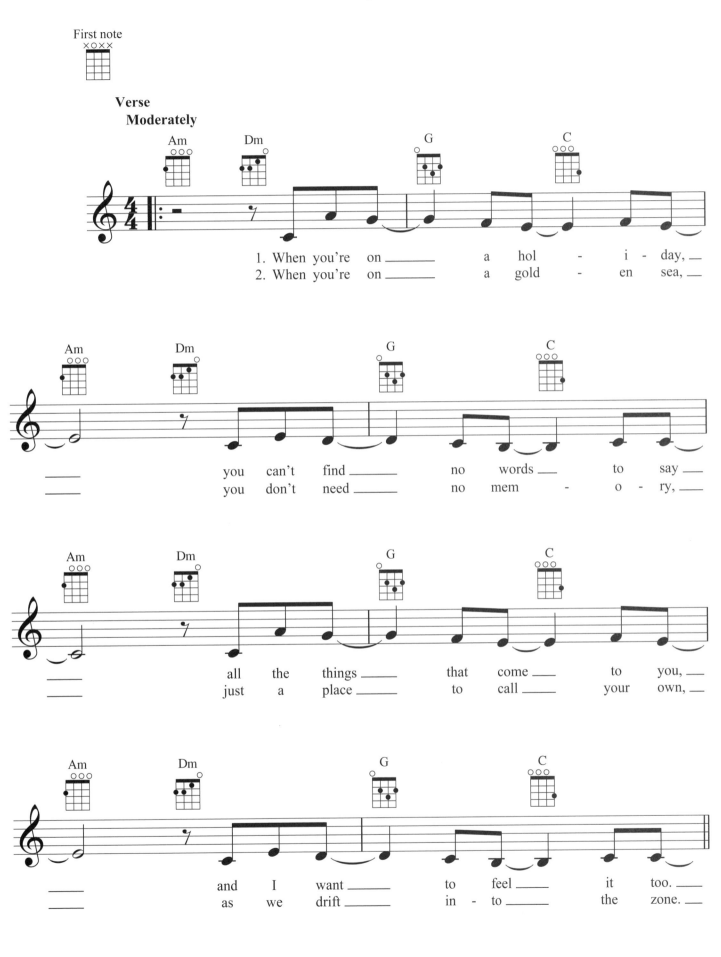

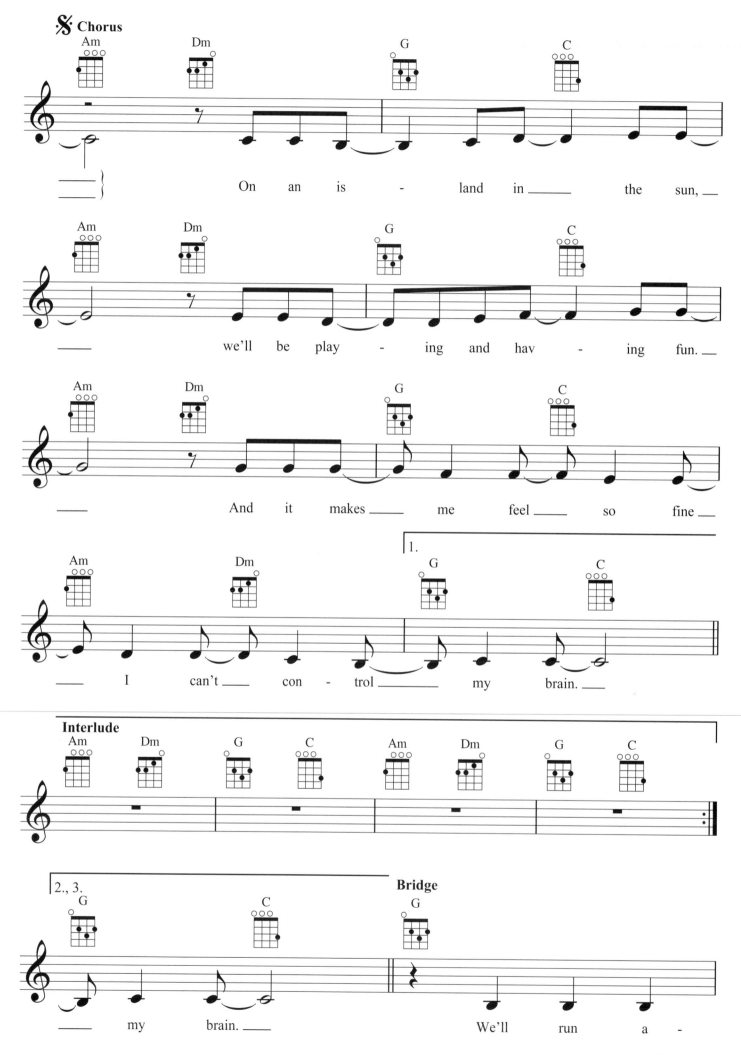

I Will Wait

Words and Music by Mumford & Sons

Iris

from the Motion Picture CITY OF ANGELS
Words and Music by John Rzeznik

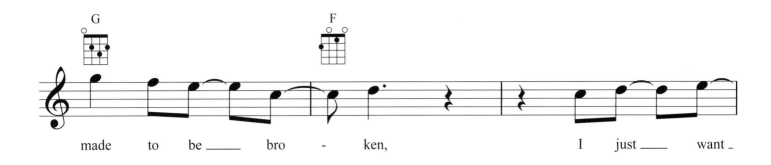

made   to   be ____ bro - ken,   I   just ____   want _

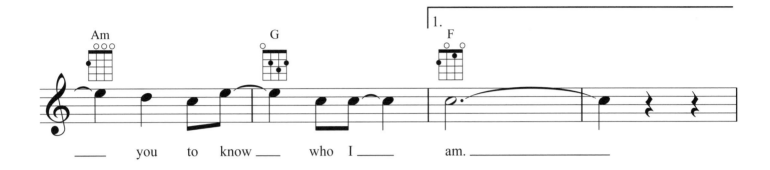

1.

____   you   to   know ____   who   I ____   am. ____

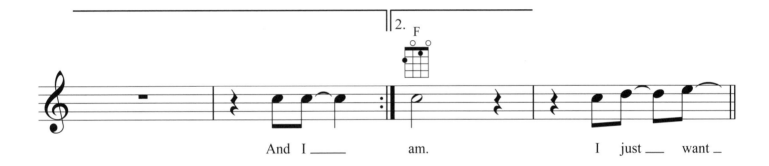

2.

And   I ____   am.   I   just ___   want _

Outro

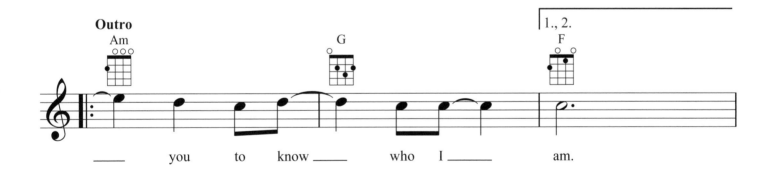

1., 2.

____   you   to   know ____   who   I ____   am.

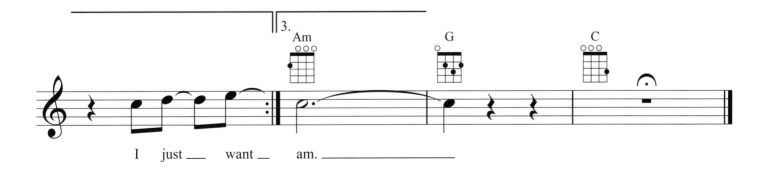

3.

I   just ___   want _   am. ____

Jack and Diane

Words and Music by John Mellencamp

Interlude

(Instrumental)

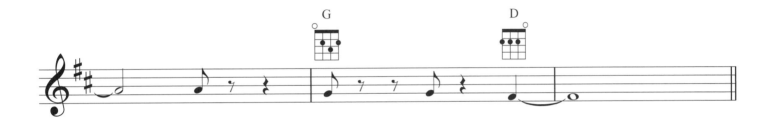

Verse

2. Suck - in'   on   a   chil - li   dog   out -
3. Jack - y   sits   back,   col - lects   his

side   the   Tast - ee   Freez. _____
thoughts   for   a ____   mo - ment,

Di - ane's   sit - tin' on
scratch - es   his

Jack - y's   lap; ____   he's   got   his   hands   be - tween ____   her   knees.
head   and   does ____   his   best   James ____   Dean:

oh yeah, _____ life _____ goes on, _____

_____

long af - ter the thrill of

To Coda ⊕ | 1.

Interlude

liv - in' is _____ gone. They walk on. *(Instrumental)*

Drums only (chords implied by vocal harmony)

4. A lit - tle dit - ty

a - bout Jack and Di - ane,

two A - mer - i - can kids do - in' the

best that they ___ can.

(Instrumental)

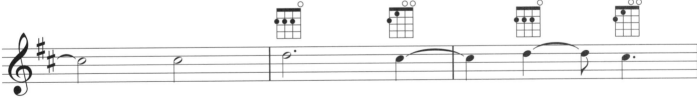

Repeat and fade

Learning to Fly

Words and Music by Tom Petty and Jeff Lynne

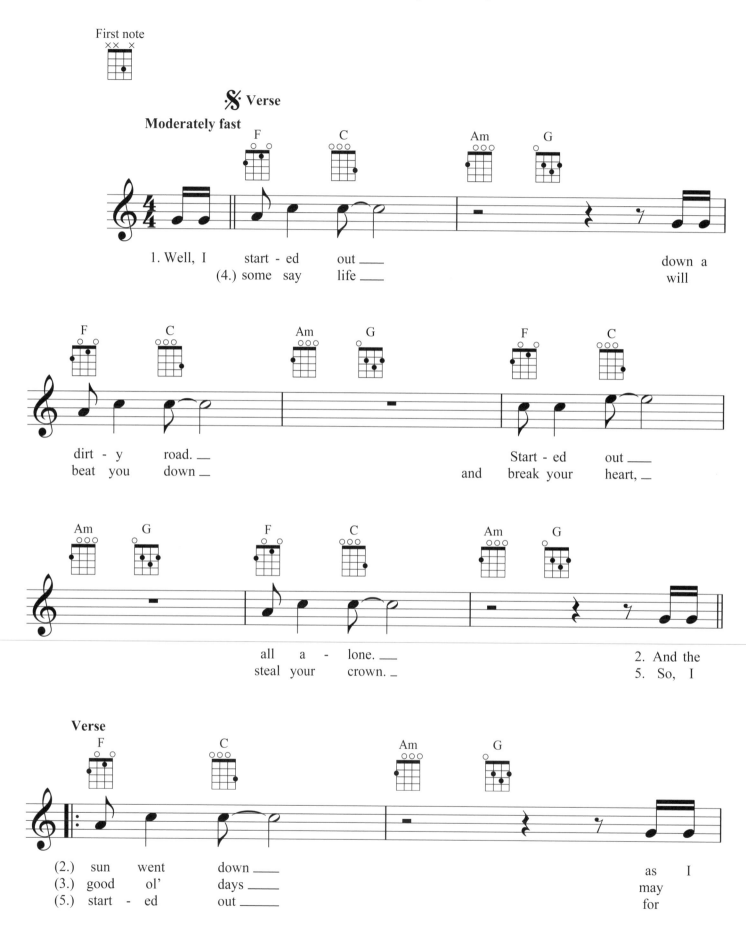

Listen to the Music

Words and Music by Tom Johnston

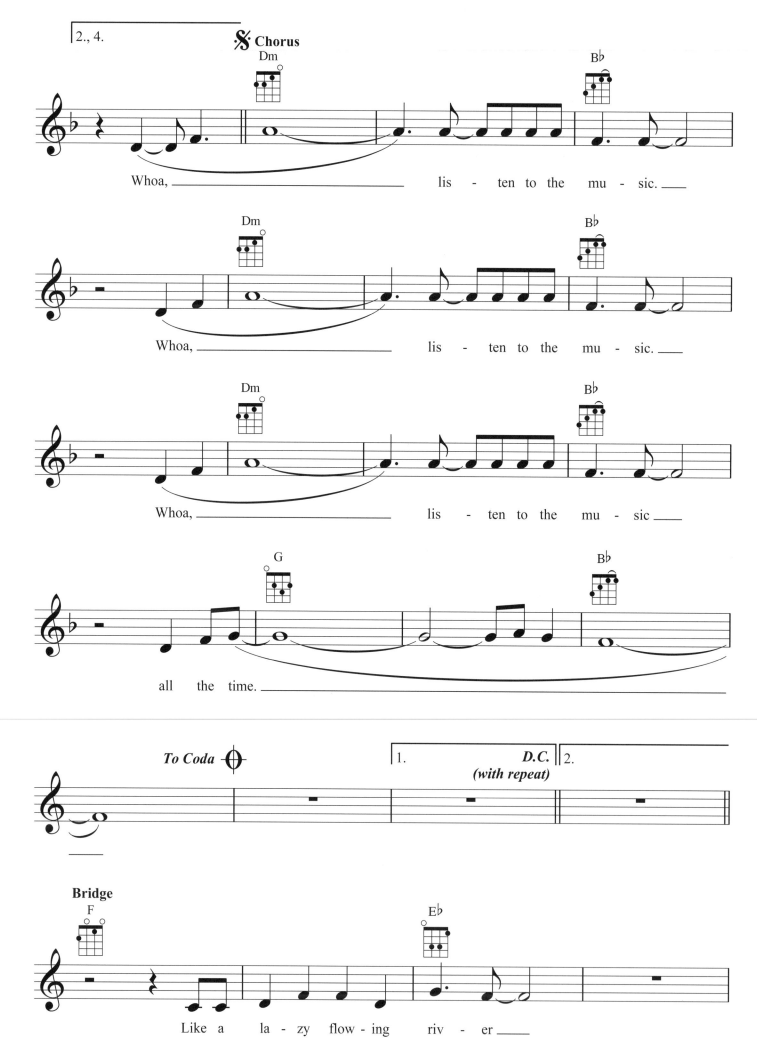

Whoa, _____ lis - ten to the mu - sic. _____

Whoa, _____ lis - ten to the mu - sic. _____

Whoa, _____ lis - ten to the mu - sic _____

all the time. _____

To Coda θ

1.

D.C.
(with repeat)

2.

Bridge

F

E♭

Like a la - zy flow - ing riv - er _____

Additional Lyrics

2. What the people need is a way to make them smile.
   It ain't so hard to do if you know how.
   Got to get a message, get it on through.
   Oh, now mama's going to after 'while.

3. Well, I know you know better everything I say.
   Meet me in the country for a day.
   We'll be happy and we'll dance.
   Oh, we're gonna dance our blues away.

4. If I'm feeling good to you and you're feeling good to me,
   There ain't nothing we can't do or say.
   Feeling good, feeling fine.
   Oh, baby, let the music play.

Losing My Religion

Words and Music by William Berry, Peter Buck, Michael Mills and Michael Stipe

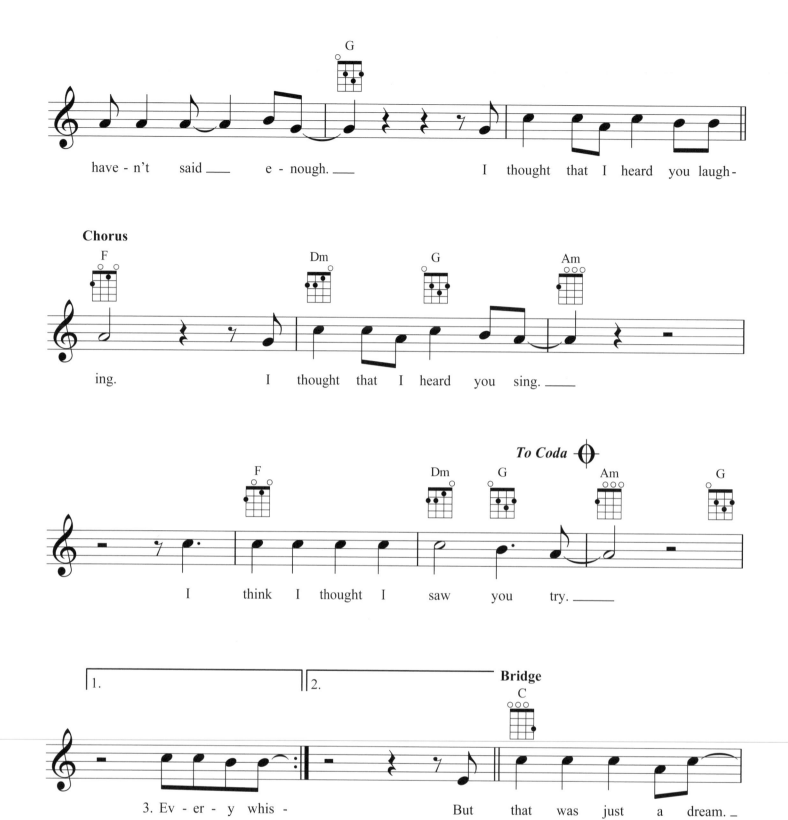

have - n't said ___ e - nough. ___   I thought that I heard you laugh-

Chorus

ing.   I thought that I heard you sing. ___

To Coda

I   think   I   thought   I   saw   you   try. ___

1.   2.   **Bridge**

3. Ev - er - y whis -   But   that   was   just   a   dream. _

D.S. al Coda

___   That   was   just   a   dream. ___ 5. That's   me   in   the   cor-

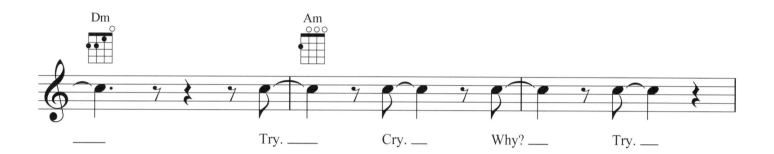

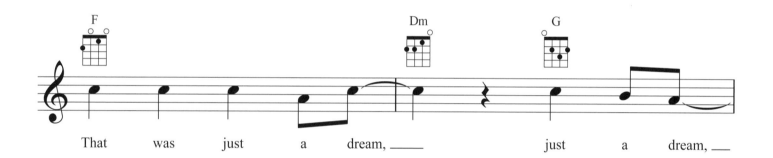

Additional Lyrics

3. Every whisper of ev'ry waking hour,
   I'm choosing my confessions,
   Trying to keep an eye on you like a hurt, lost and blinded fool.
   Oh no, I've said too much. I set it up.

4. Consider this, consider this the hint of the century.
   Consider this: the slip that brought me to my knees failed.
   What if all these fantasies come flailing around?
   And now I've said too much.

Maggie May

Words and Music by Rod Stewart and Martin Quittenton

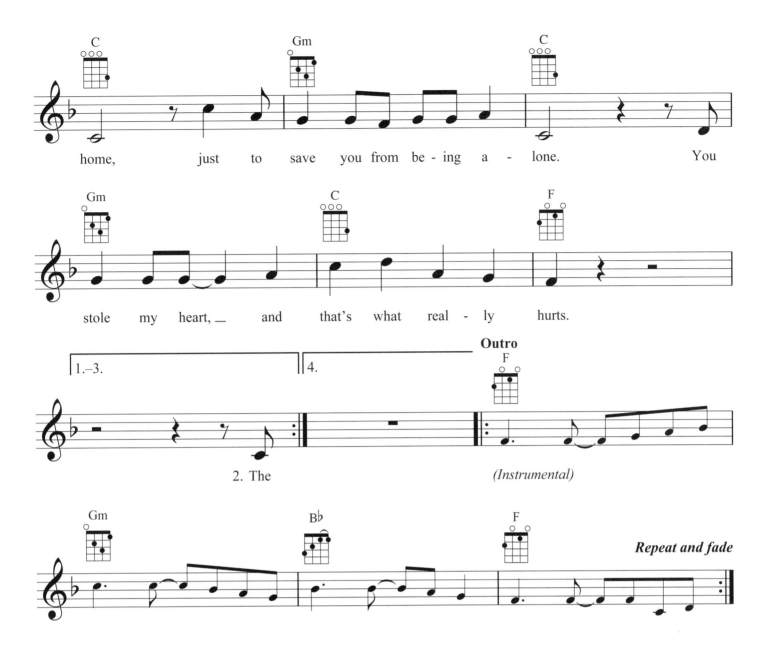

home, just to save you from be-ing a-lone. You

stole my heart, — and that's what real-ly hurts.

Outro

2. The

(Instrumental)

Repeat and fade

Additional Lyrics

2. The morning sun, when it's in your face,
   Really shows your age.
   But that don't worry me none;
   In my eyes, you're everything.
   I laughed at all of your jokes.
   My love you didn't need to coax.
   Oh, Maggie, I couldn't have tried any more.

Chorus: You led me away from home
   Just to save you from being alone.
   You stole my soul,
   And that's a pain I can do without.

3. All I needed was a friend
   To lend a guiding hand.
   But you turned into a lover and, mother, what a lover!
   You wore me out.
   All you did was wreck my bed,
   And in the morning, kick me in the head.
   Oh, Maggie, I couldn't have tried any more.

Chorus: You led me away from home
   'Cause you didn't want to be alone.
   You stole my heart;
   I couldn't leave you if I tried.

4. I suppose I could collect my books
   And get on back to school,
   Or steal my daddy's cue
   And make a living out of playing pool.
   Or find myself a rock 'n' roll band
   That needs a helping hand.
   Oh, Maggie, I wish I'd never seen your face.

Chorus: You made a first-class fool out of me,
   But I'm as blind as a fool can be.
   You stole my heart, but I love you anyway.

Morning Has Broken

Words by Eleanor Farjeon
Music by Cat Stevens

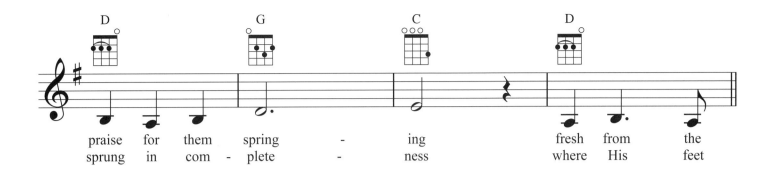

praise   for   them   spring   -   ing
sprung   in   com - plete   -   ness

fresh   where   from   the
from   His   the   feet

Interlude

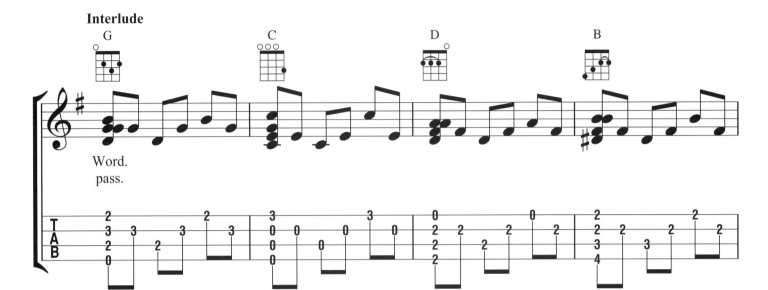

Word.
pass.

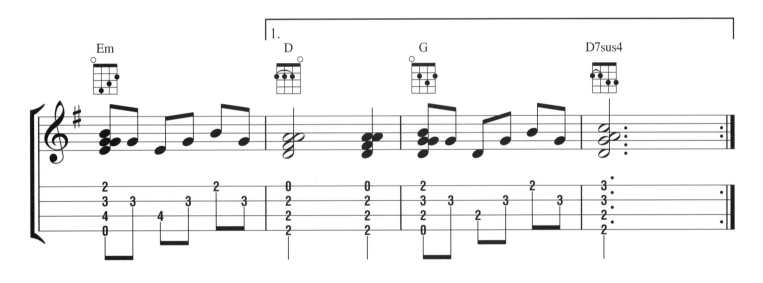

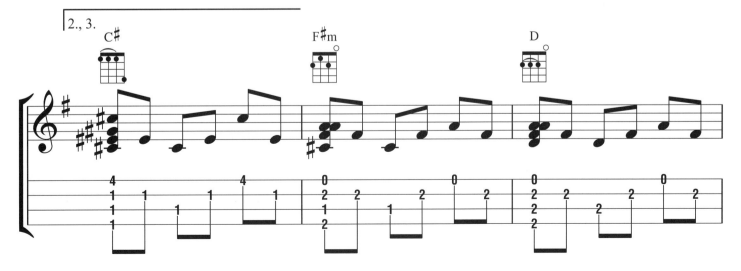

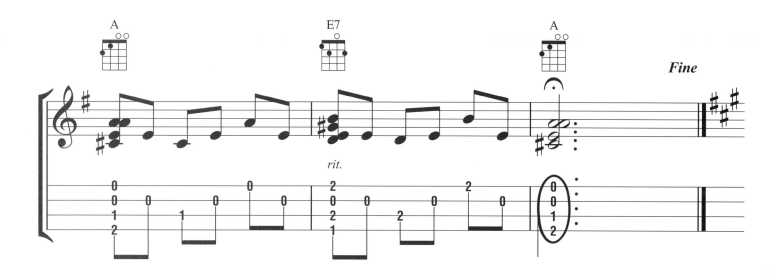

Fine

Verse

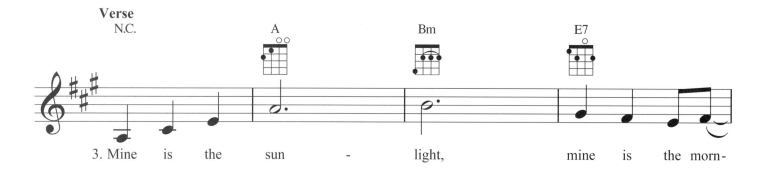

3. Mine is the sun - light, mine is the morn-

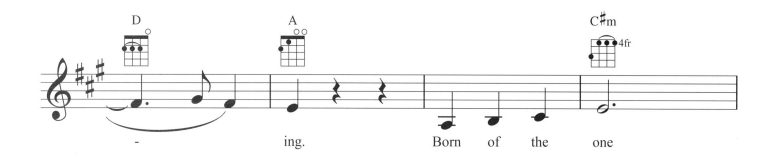

- ing. Born of the one

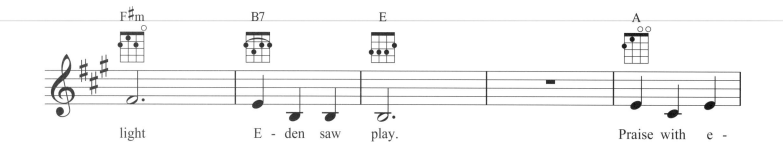

light E - den saw play. Praise with e -

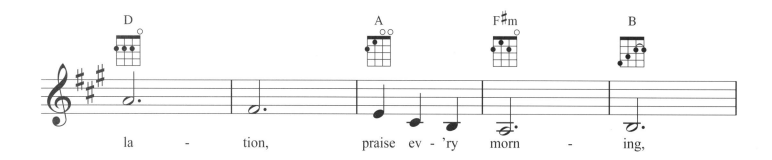

la - tion, praise ev - 'ry morn - ing,

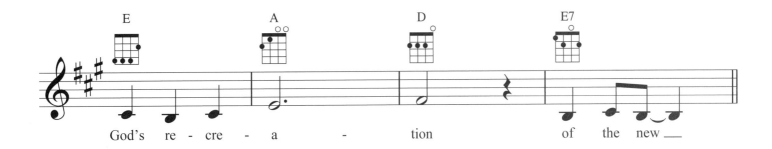

God's re - cre - a - tion of the new __

Interlude

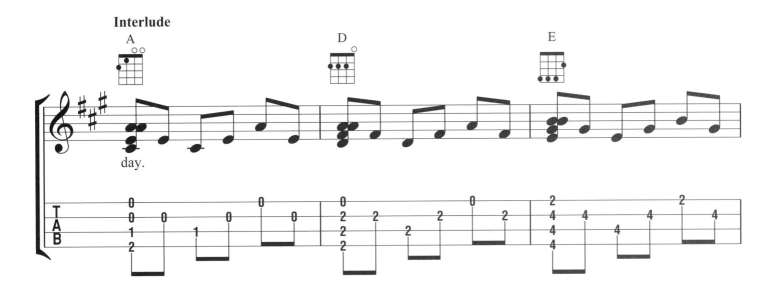

day.

D.C. al Fine
(take 2nd ending)

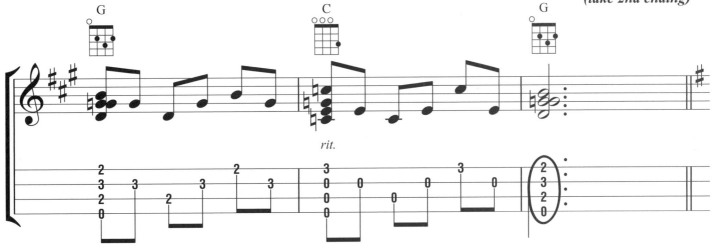

rit.

117

Night Moves

Words and Music by Bob Seger

1. I was a lit-tle too tall, could-a used a few pounds.

Tight pants, points, hard - ly re - nown.

She was a black - haired _ beau-ty with big, dark eyes _____

and points all her own _ sit - tin' way up high, _

way up firm and high. _____

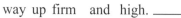

Out past the corn - fields where the woods ___ got heav - y,

out in the back seat of my Six - ty Chev - y,

work - in' ___ on mys - t'ries with - out ___ an - y clues. ___

Chorus

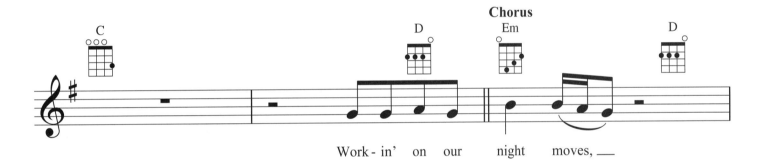

Work - in' on our night moves, ___

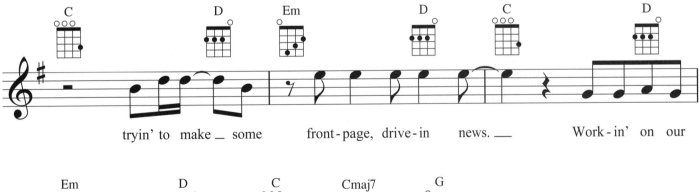

tryin' to make ___ some front - page, drive - in news. ___ Work - in' on our

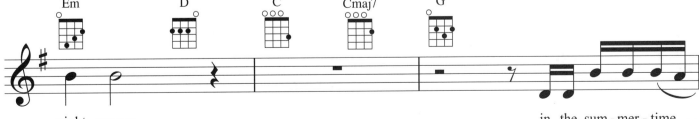

night moves in the sum - mer - time, ___

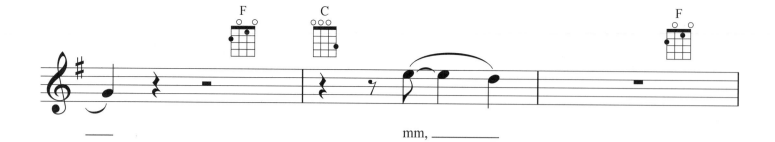

mm, _____

in the sweet __ sum - mer - time. _____

Verse

2. We weren't in love. Oh, no, far from it.

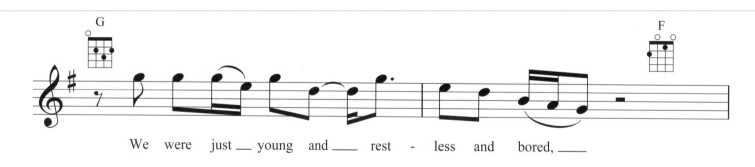

We weren't search - in' for some pie - in - the - sky sum - mit.

We were just __ young and __ rest - less and bored, _____

liv - ing by the sword. _____

And we'd steal a - way ev - 'ry chance we could

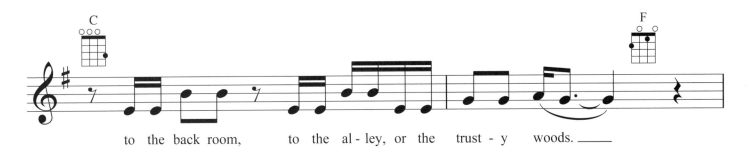

to the back room, to the al - ley, or the trust - y woods. ____

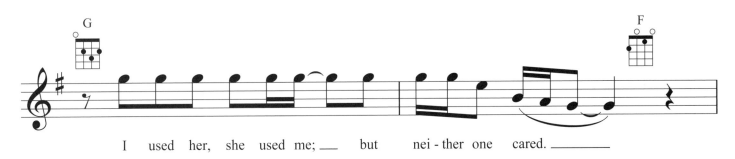

I used her, she used me; ___ but nei - ther one cared. ____

Chorus

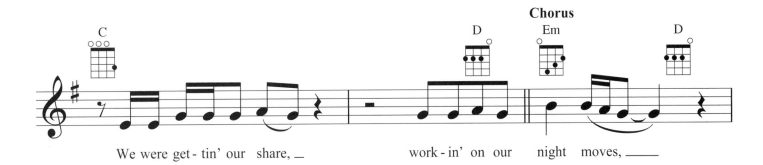

We were get - tin' our share, ___ work - in' on our night moves, ____

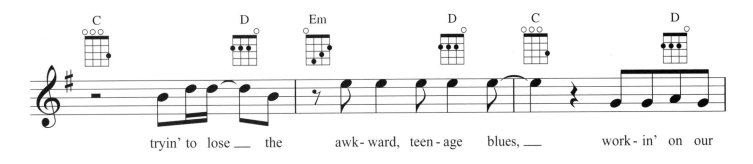

tryin' to lose ___ the awk - ward, teen - age blues, ___ work - in' on our

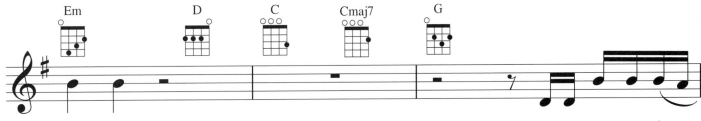

night moves. It was sum - mer - time, ___

No Woman No Cry

Words and Music by Vincent Ford

Additional Lyrics

2. Said, I remember when we used to sit
   In the government yard in Trenchtown.
   And then Georgie would make a firelight
   As it was log wood burnin' through the night.
   Then we would cook cornmeal porridge,
   Of which I'll share with you.
   My feet is my only carriage,
   So, I've got to push on through.
   But while I'm gone, I mean...

Party Favor

Words and Music by Billie Eilish O'Connell and Finneas O'Connell

Patience

Words and Music by W. Axl Rose, Slash, Izzy Stradlin', Duff McKagan and Steven Adler

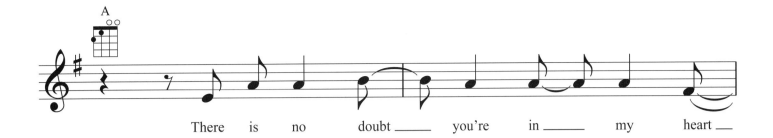

There is no doubt _____ you're in _____ my heart _____

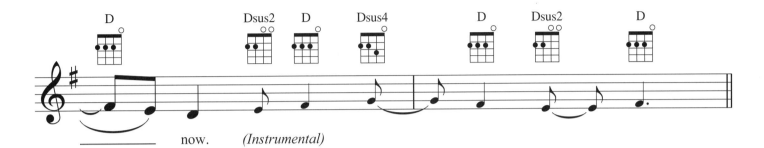

_____ now.   *(Instrumental)*

Chorus

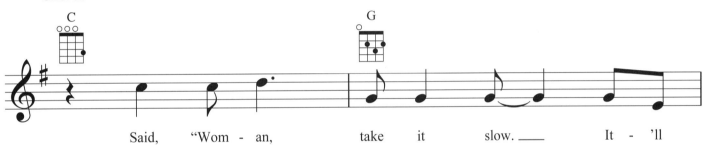

Said, "Wom - an,   take it   slow. _____   It - 'll

work   it - self _____   out   fine. _____

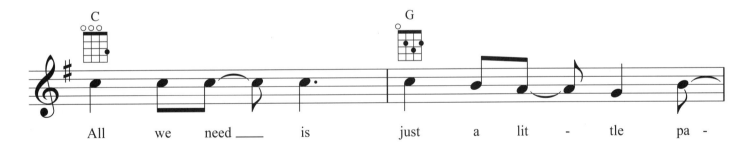

All   we   need _____   is   just   a   lit - tle   pa -

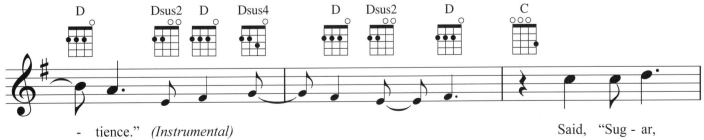

- tience."   *(Instrumental)*   Said, "Sug - ar,

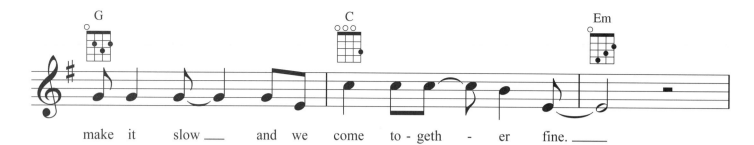

make it slow ___ and we come to - geth - er fine. _____

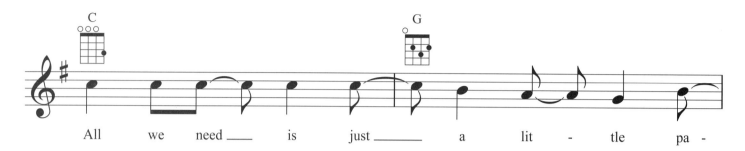

All we need ___ is just _____ a lit - tle pa -

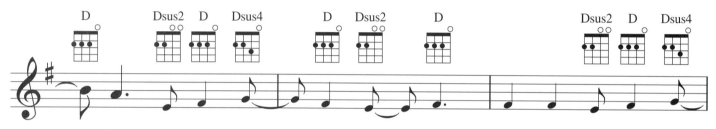

- tience." *(Instrumental)*

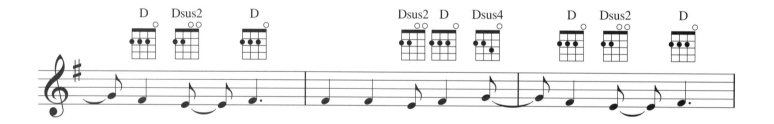

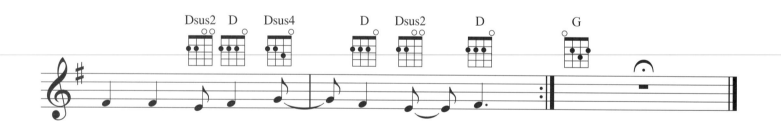

Additional Lyrics

2. I sit here on the stairs 'cause I'd rather be alone.
If I can't have you right now, I'll wait, dear.
Sometimes I get so tense, but I can't speed up the time.
But you know, love, there's one more thing to consider.

Chorus: Said, "Woman, take it slow, and things will be just fine.
You and I'll just use a little patience."
Said, "Sugar, take the time 'cause the lights are shining bright.
You and I've got what it takes to make it.
We won't fake it.
Ah, I'll never break it.
'Cause I can't take it."

Photograph

Lyrics by Chad Kroeger
Music by Nickelback

D

And this is where I went ___ to school.
We used to lis - ten to the ra - di - o

A

Most of the time, had bet - ter things to do.
and sing a - long with ev - 'ry song we'd know.

Cadd9

Crim - i - nal rec - ord says I broke in twice;
We said some - day we'd find out how it twice feels

G

I must have done it half a doz - en times.
to sing to more than just the steer - ing wheel.

D

I won - der if it's ___ too late.
Kim's the first girl I kissed.

A

Should I go back and try to grad - u - ate?
I was so nerv - ous that I near - ly missed.

Life's bet - ter now than it was _____ back then.
She's had a cou - ple of kids _____ since then.

If I was them, I would - n't let me in. _____
I have - n't seen her since God knows when. ____

Oh, _____ whoa, _____ whoa, oh, God, I, _____ I... Ev - 'ry

𝄋 Chorus

mem - o - ry of look - ing out the back door, I had the

pho - to al - bum spread out on my bed - room floor. It's

hard to say it, time to say it: Good - bye, _____ good - bye. Ev - 'ry

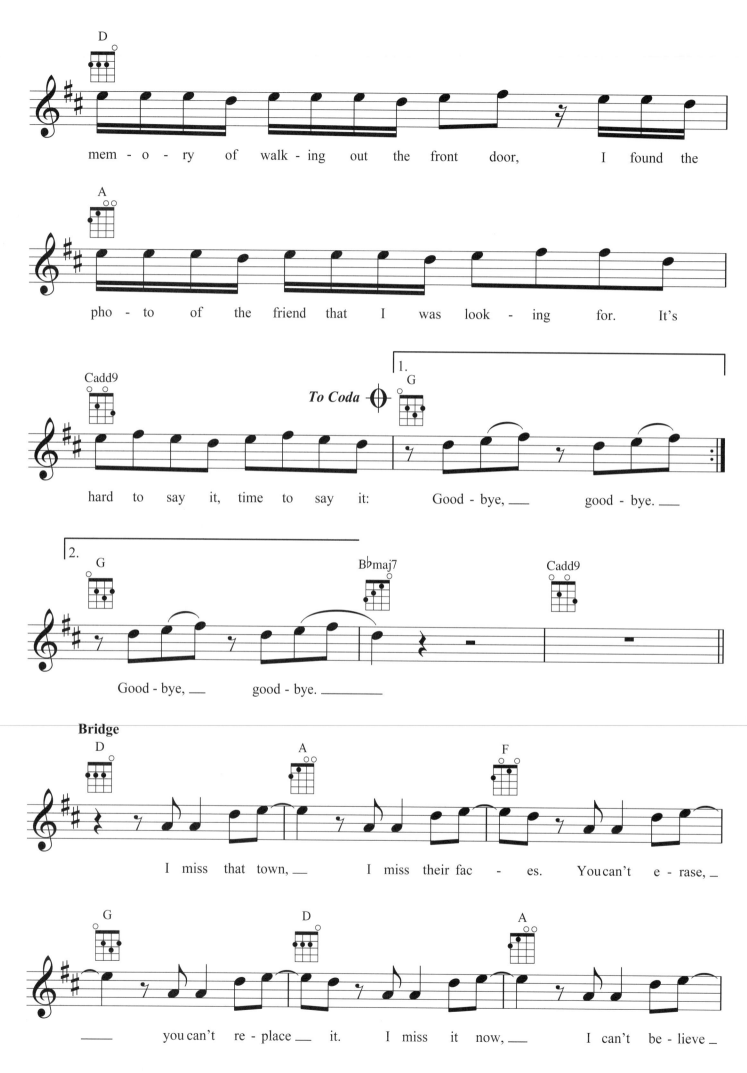

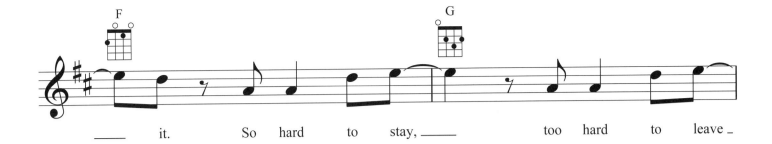

_____ it.   So hard   to   stay, _____   too hard   to   leave ___

_____ it.   If   I   could   re - live ____   those   days, ___

____   I know the one thing that would nev - er   change. ___   Ev -'ry_

_Good - bye, ___   good - bye. _____   Look at this pho - to - graph. ____

____   Ev - 'ry   time   I   do,   it   makes   me   laugh. ____

____   Ev -'ry time I do, it makes me..._

Rocky Mountain High

Words and Music by John Denver and Mike Taylor

you might say he found a key _____ for ev - 'ry door. _
and he lost a friend but kept his mem - o - ry. _____

𝄋 **Verse**

2. When he first came to the moun -
4. Now he walks in qui - et sol -
(5.) _____ is full of won -

- tains, _____ his life _ was far a - way, _____ on the road _
- i - tude, the for - ests and the streams _ seek - ing
- der _____ but his heart _ still knows some fear _____ of a

and hang - in' by a song. _____
grace _____ in ev - 'ry step he takes. _____
sim - ple thing he can - not com - pre - hend: _____

But the string's al - read - y bro - ken and he
His sight _____ has turned in - side _____ him - self to
Why they try to tear the moun - tains down to

139

-light _____ is soft- er than a lull - a - by. _____
lis - ten to the cas - u - al _____ re - ply. _____
-er man _ if he nev- er saw an ea - gle fly. _____

Rock - y Moun - tain high. _

(Instrumental)

To Coda

Rock - y Moun - tain high. _____ (Instrumental)

1. **2.** ***D.S. al Coda***

3. He climbed _ 5. Now his life _

Runaway Train

Words and Music by David Pirner

First note

Verse
Moderately

1. Call you up in the mid - dle of the night,
2. Can you help me re - mem - ber how to smile?

like a fi - re - fly with - out a light. __ You were there like a
Make it, some - how, all seem worth - while. __ How on earth did I

blow - torch burn - ing; I was a key that could use a lit - tle turn - ing. __
get so jad - ed? Life's mys - ter - y seems _____ so fad - ed. __

So tired that I could - n't e - ven sleep, so man - y se - crets
I can go where no one else can go. I know what no

I could - n't keep. __ Prom - ised my - self I would - n't weep.
one else knows. Here I am just drown - in' in the rain

one - way track. __ Seems like I should be get - ting some - where.

Some - how I'm nei - ther here nor there. ____ 3. Bought a tick - et for a

run - a - way train, like a mad man laugh - in' at the rain; __

lit - tle out of touch, lit - tle in - sane. Just eas - i - er than

deal - ing with the pain. ____

here nor there. ____

The Scientist

Words and Music by Guy Berryman, Jon Buckland, Will Champion and Chris Martin

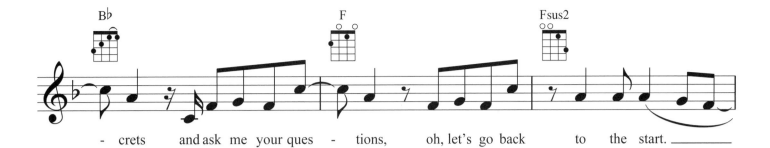

- crets   and ask me your ques - tions,   oh, let's go back   to   the start. _____

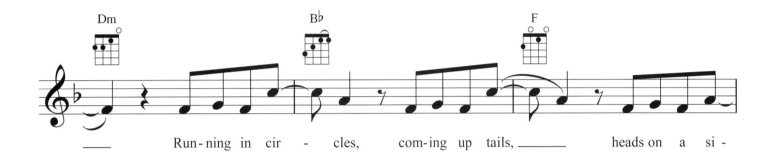

_____   Run-ning in cir - cles,   com-ing up tails, _____   heads on a si -

Chorus

- lence   a - part. _____   No - bod - y said ___ it was eas - y. _____

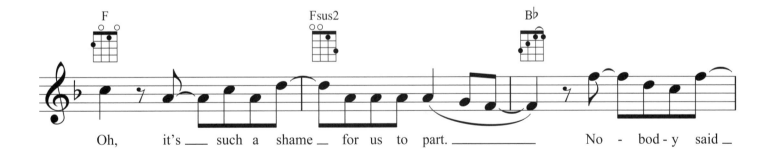

_____   it was eas - y. _____   Oh,   it's ___ such a shame ___ for us to part. _____   No - bod - y said ___

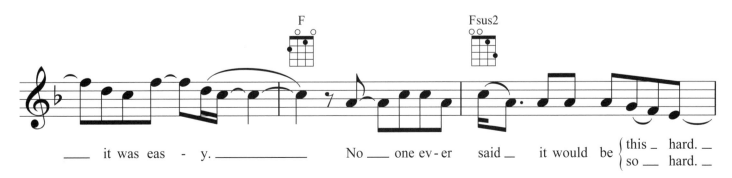

_____   it was eas - y. _____   No ___ one ev - er said ___ it would be { this ___ hard. _
                                                                                 { so ___ hard. _

147

Oh, take me } back to the start. _____
I'm go-ing }

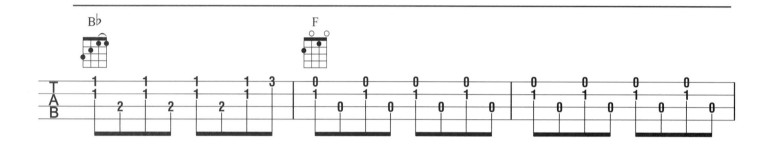

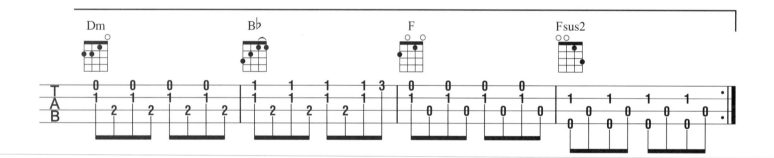

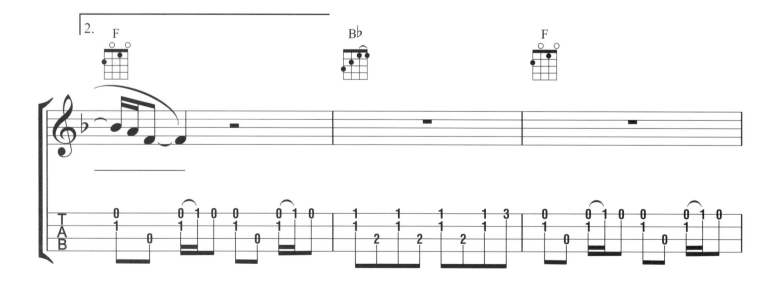

148

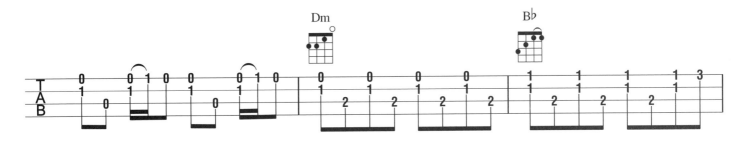

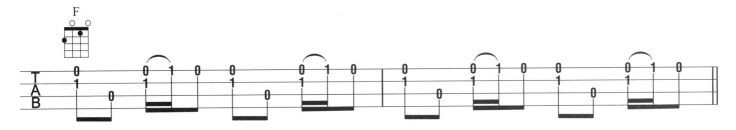

Outro

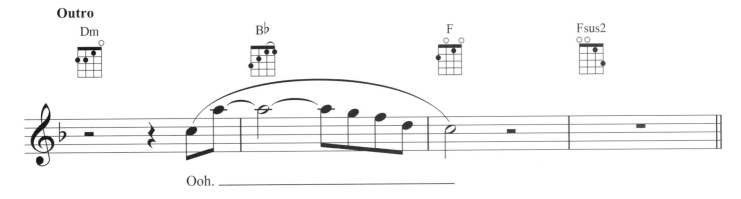

Ooh.

Ah   ooh.

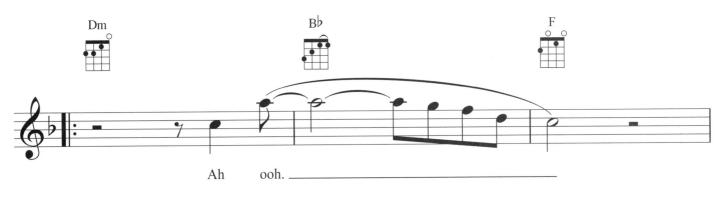

Ah   ooh.

Additional Lyrics

2. I was just guessing at numbers and figures,
   Pulling the puzzles apart.
   Questions of science, science and progress
   Do not speak as loud as my heart.
   And tell me you love me, come back and haunt me.
   Oh, and I rush to the start.
   Running in circles, chasing our tails,
   Coming back as we are.

Southern Cross

Words and Music by Stephen Stills, Richard Curtis and Michael Curtis

First note

Verse
Moderately slow, in 2

1. Got out of town ____ on a boat ____ goin' to south-ern is - lands, sail-ing a reach be - fore a fol-low-ing sea.

She was mak-in' for the trades ____ on the out-side, and the down-hill run

to Pa - pe - 'e - te.   2. Off the wind ___

Verse

___   on this head - ing lie ___ the Mar - que - sas.
(4.) sail - ing for to - mor - row; my dreams are a - dy - ing.

We got eight - y feet ___ of the wa - ter - line
And my love is an an - chor tied to you,

nice - ly mak - in' way.   In a nois - y bar ___ in
tied with a sil - ver chain. I have my ship,   and

Av - a - lon I tried to call you,   but on the
all her flags are a - fly - ing.   She is

mid - night watch I re - al - ized why twice you ran a - way. ___
all that I have left, and Mu - sic is her name. ___

Pre-Chorus

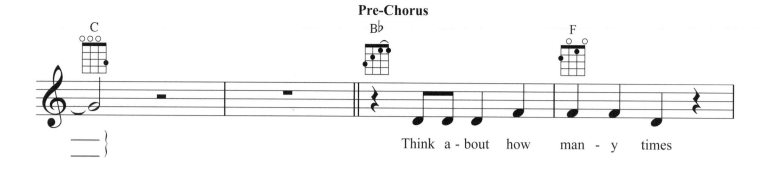

Think a-bout how man-y times

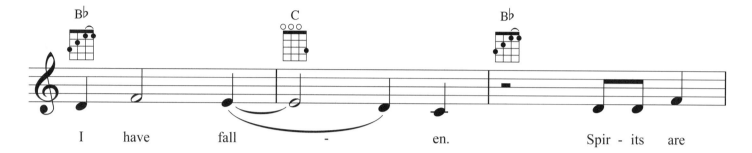

I have fall - en. Spir - its are

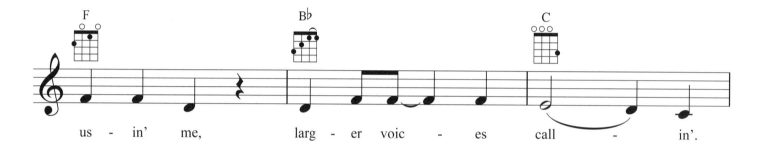

us - in' me, larg - er voic - es call - in'.

What heav - en brought you and me can-not be for-got-

- ten. I have been a-

Chorus

round _____ the world,

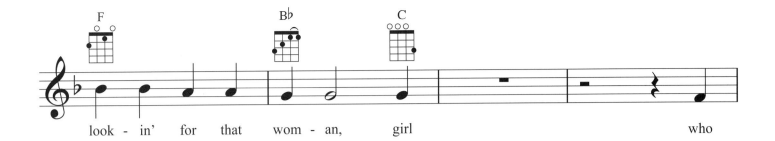

look - in' for that wom - an, girl who

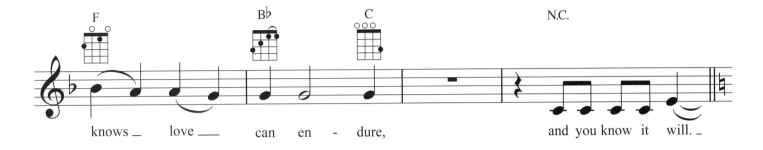

knows ___ love ___ can en - dure, and you know it will. ___

Interlude

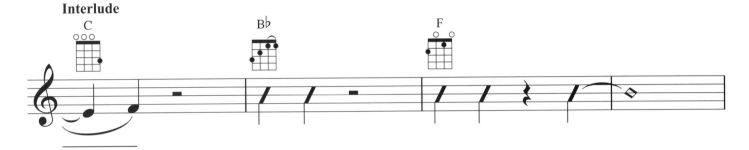

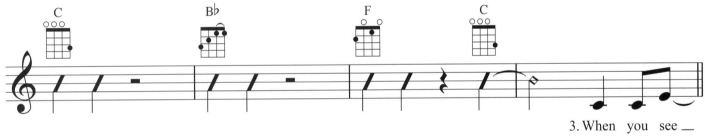

3. When you see ___
5. So we cheat -

Verse

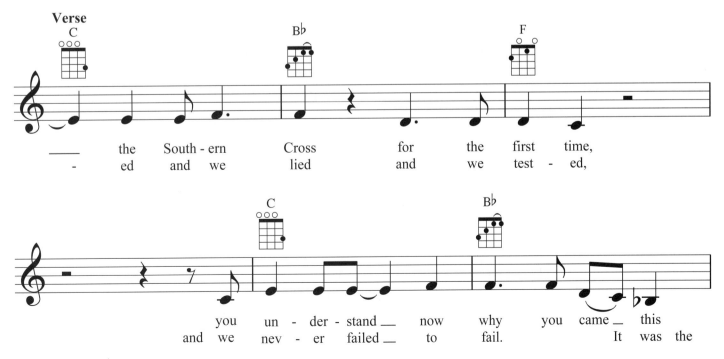

___ the South - ern Cross for the first time,
- ed and we lied for and we test - ed,

you un - der - stand ___ now why you came ___ this
and we nev - er failed ___ to fail. It was the

way.
eas - i - est thing to do.

'Cause the truth you might ___ be
You will ___ sur -

run - nin' from is so small,
vive be - ing best - ed.

but it's as
Some - bod - y

big as the prom - ise,
fine will come a - long, make me for - get a - bout lov - in'

the prom - ise of a com - in'

1. N.C.

2.

day.
you

4. So ___ I'm

in the South - ern

Outro

Cross.

She Talks to Angels

Words and Music by Chris Robinson and Rich Robinson

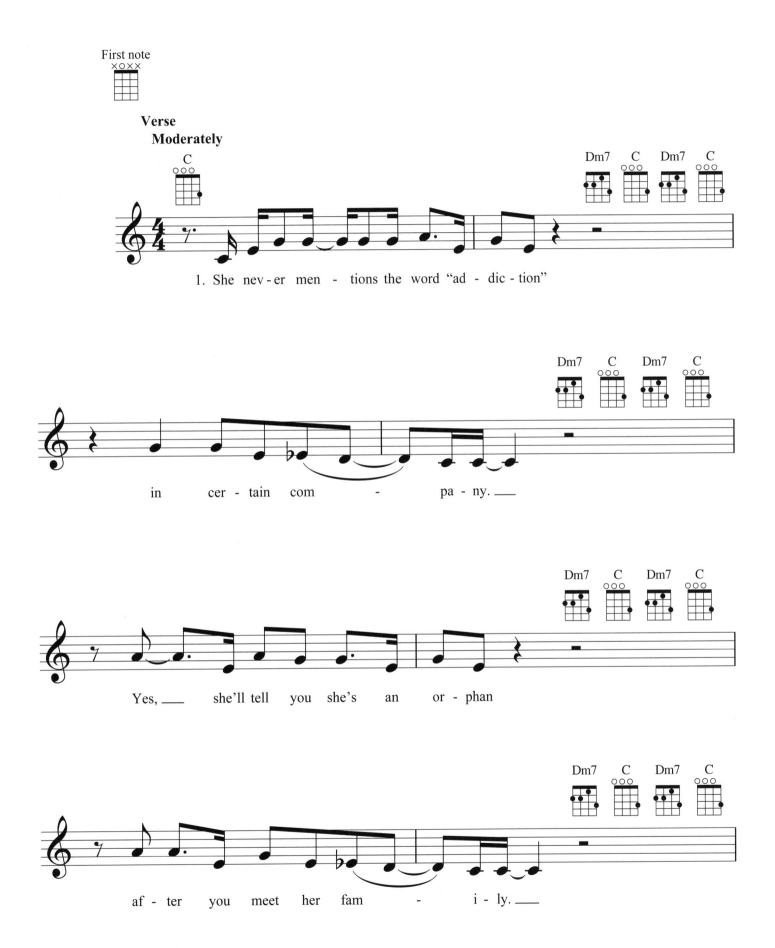

1. She nev - er men - tions the word "ad - dic - tion"

in cer - tain com - pa - ny. ___

Yes, ___ she'll tell you she's an or - phan

af - ter you meet her fam - i - ly. ___

%. **Verse**

2. She paints her eyes as black as night, now.
(3.) pock - et.

Pulls those shades _ down _____ tight.
She wears a cross a - round her neck.

Yeah, _ she gives a smile _____ when the pain _ comes.
Yes, _____ the hair is ____ from a lit - tle boy,

The pain gon - na make ev - 'ry - thing al - right. _____
and the cross is from some - one she has not met, not yet. _

Chorus

Says she talks to an - gels, _____

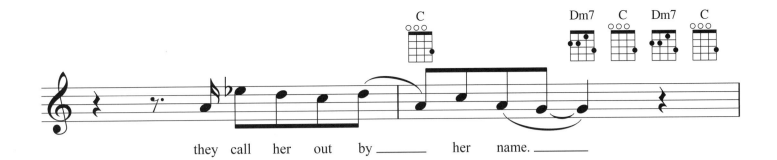

they call her out by _____ her name. _____

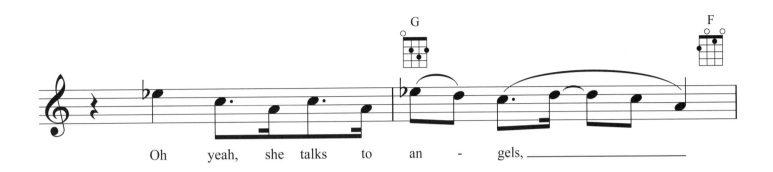

Oh yeah, she talks to an - gels, _____

To Coda

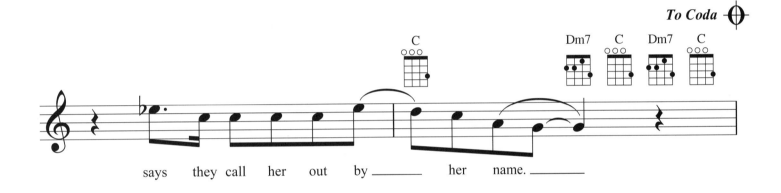

says they call her out by _____ her name. _____

3. She keeps a lock of hair in her

Bridge

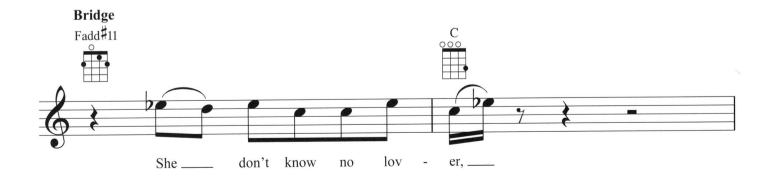

She _____ don't know no lov - er, _____

157

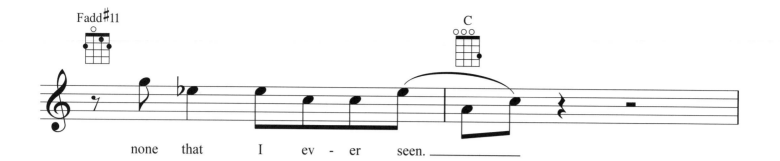

none that I ev - er seen. ___

And to her ___ that ain't noth - in', ___ but to me

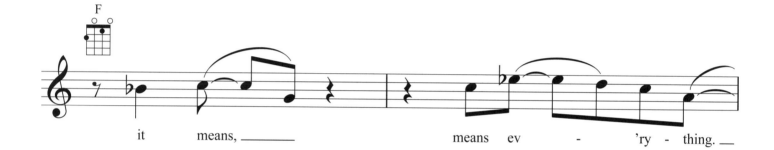

it means, ___ means ev - 'ry - thing. ___

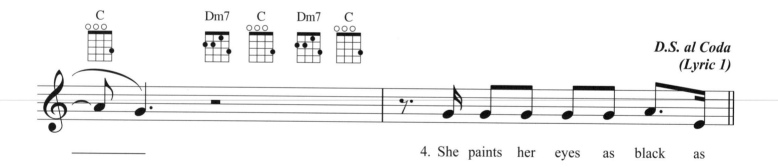

D.S. al Coda
(Lyric 1)

___ 4. She paints her eyes as black as

Oh, ___ an - gels, ___

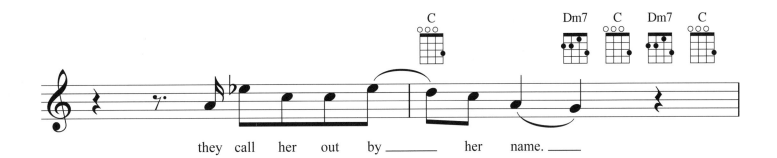

they call her out by _____ her name. _____

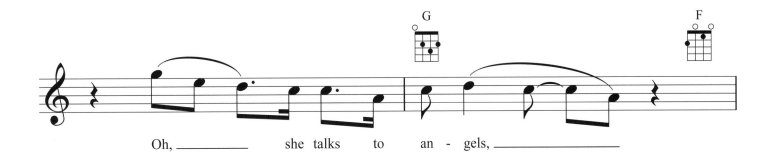

Oh, _____ she talks to an - gels, _____

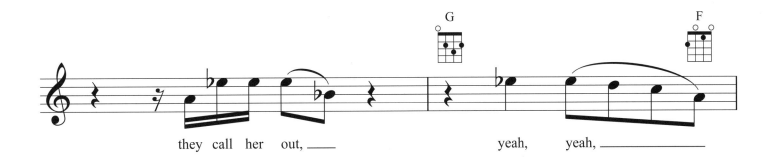

they call her out, _____ yeah, yeah, _____

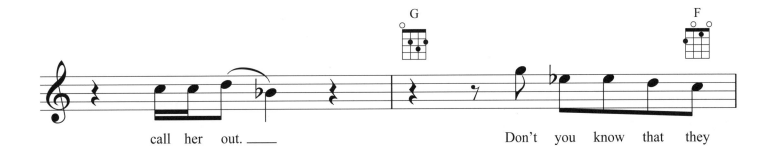

call her out. _____ Don't you know that they

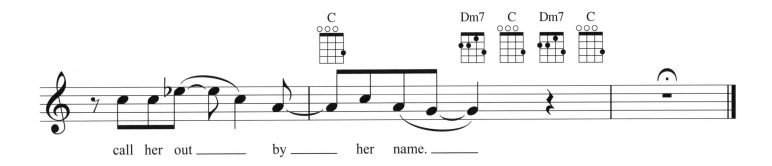

call her out _____ by _____ her name. _____

Teardrops on My Guitar

Words and Music by Taylor Swift and Liz Rose

To Be with You

Words and Music by Eric Martin and David Grahame

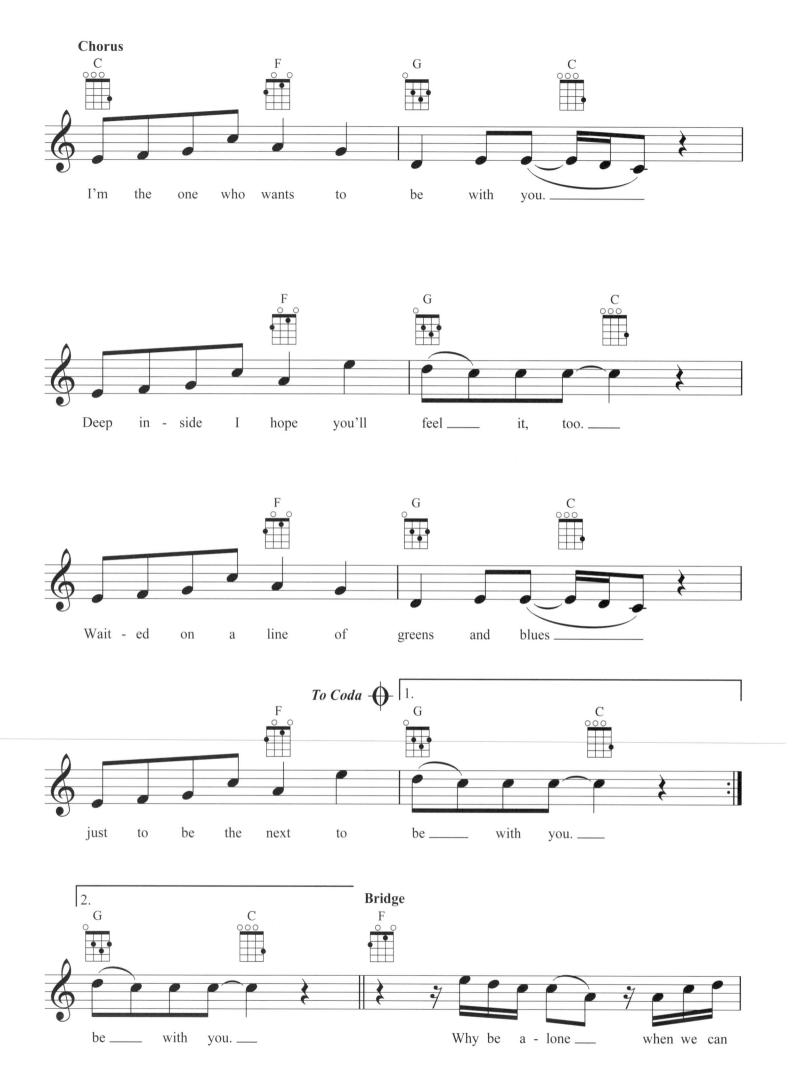

Time for Me to Fly

Words and Music by Kevin Cronin

Chorus

steal - in' your love _____ a - way 'cause you nev - er give _____
nough of the false - ness of a worn - out re - la -

_____ it; peel - in' the years _____ a - way, and
- tion e - nough of the jeal - ous - y and the

we can't re - live _____ it. }
in - tol - er - a - tion. }   I make you laugh, _

_____ and _ you make me cry. _____

I be - lieve it's time _____ for me _ to fly. _____

1.

Wish You Were Here

Words and Music by Roger Waters and David Gilmour

1. So, _____ so you think you can tell _____
2. *See additional lyrics*

heav - en from hell, _____

blue skies _ from pain? _ Can you tell a green _

field _____ from a cold, steel rail, _____

a smile _ from a veil? Do you think you can tell? _

Chorus

Did they get you to trade

your he - roes for ghosts, ___ hot ash - es for trees, __

hot air ___ for a cool ___ breeze, __

cold _ com - fort for charge? ___ And did you ___ ex - change _

___ a walk - on part ___ in the war ___ for a lead _

___ role in a cage? ___ *(Instrumental)*

Interlude

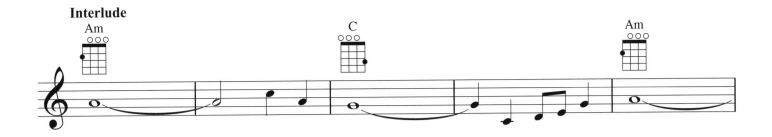

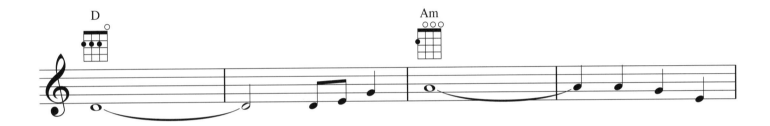

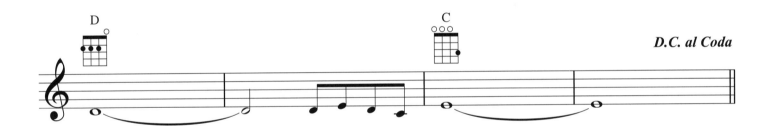

D.C. al Coda

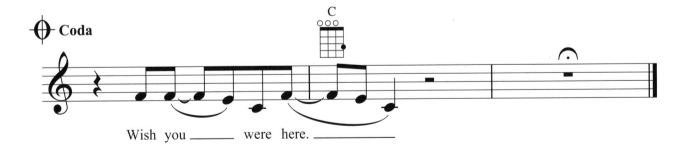

Wish you ___ were here. ___

Additional Lyrics

2. How I wish, how I wish you were here.
   We're just two lost souls swimming in a fish bowl year after year.
   Running over the same old ground, what have we found?
   The same old fears. Wish you were here.

Uncle John's Band

Words by Robert Hunter
Music by Jerry Garcia

Wanted Dead or Alive

Words and Music by Jon Bon Jovi and Richie Sambora

Additional Lyrics

2. Sometimes I sleep, sometimes it's not for days.
   The people I meet always go their separate ways.
   Sometimes you tell the day by the bottle that you drink.
   And times when you're alone, all you do is think.

3. And I walk these streets, a loaded six-string on my back.
   I play for keeps, 'cause I might not make it back.
   I've been everywhere, still I'm standing tall.
   I've seen a million faces and I've rocked them all.

What's Up

Words and Music by Linda Perry

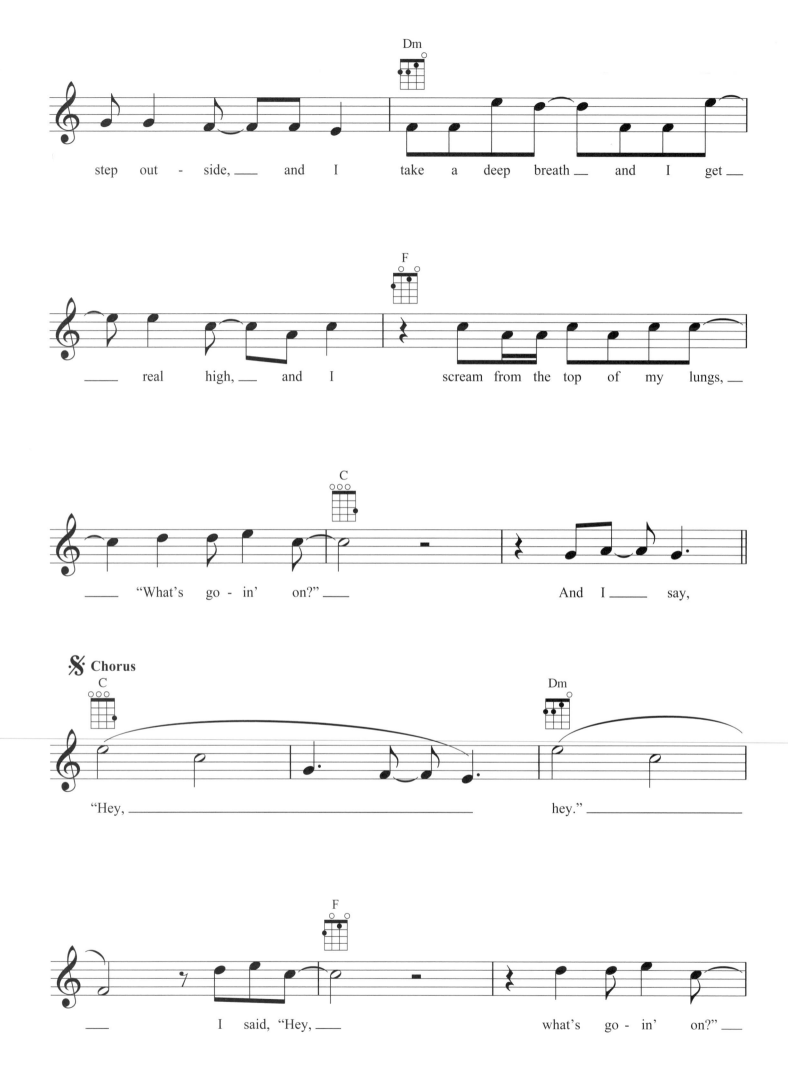

And I ___ say, "Hey, _____

_____ hey." _____ I said, "Hey, _

what's go-in' on?" ___

And I ___ say,

___

Ooh, ooh, ___ ooh, _____

ooh, _____ uh - huh.

Slower, easy Shuffle (♪♪ = ♪ ♪)

Twen - ty - five years of my

life, and still _____ I'm trying to get up that

great big hill _____ of hope _____

for a des - ti - na - tion.

Wonderful Tonight

Words and Music by Eric Clapton

1. It's late in the eve - ning;
2. We go to a par - ty,
3. It's time to go home ___ now,

she's won - d'ring what clothes ___ to wear. ___
ev - 'ry - one turns ___ to see ___
I've got an ach - ing head. ___

She puts on her make -
this beau - ti - ful la -
So I give her the car ___

- up
- dy
___ keys,

and brush - es her long, ___ blonde hair. ___
is walk - ing a - round ___ with me. ___
and she helps me to bed. ___

And then she asks ___ me,
And then she asks ___ me,
And then I tell ___ her,

"Do I look all right?" ___
"Do you feel all right?" ___
as I turn out the light, ___

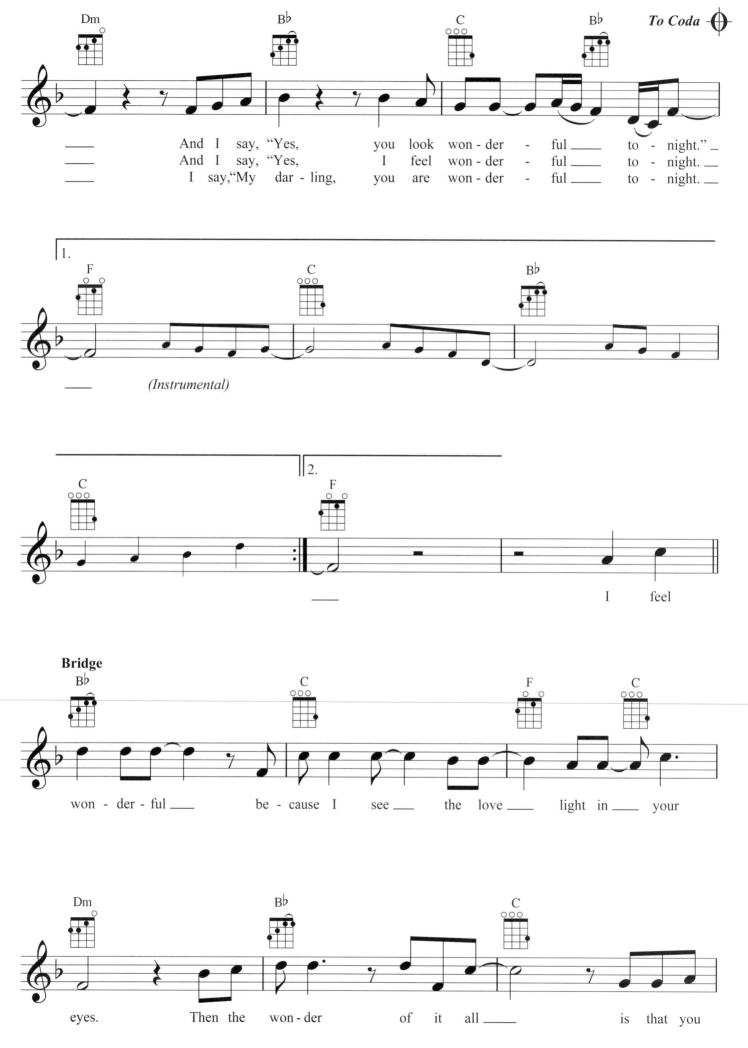

just don't re - al - ize ____ how much ___ I love ___ you." *(Instrumental)*

D.C. al Coda

Coda   **Outro**

____   Oh,   my   dar - ling,   you   are

won - der - ful _____ to - night." ___   *(Instrumental)*

You're Beautiful

Words and Music by James Blunt, Sacha Skarbek and Amanda Ghost

crowd - ed ___ place. ___   And I don't know what ___ to do, ___

To Coda ⊕

Interlude

___   'cause I'll nev - er be ___ with you. ___

2. Yes, she

Verse

caught my eye ___ as I walked on by. ___   She could

see from my face ___ that I was fly - ing high. And I ___ don't think that I'll

D.S. al Coda

see her a - gain, ___ but we shared a mo - ment that will last ___ to the end. ___

Wonderwall

Words and Music by Noel Gallagher

Additional Lyrics

2. Backbeat the word was on the street that the fire in your heart is out.
   I'm sure you've heard it all before, but you never really had a doubt.
   I don't believe that anybody feels the way I do about you now.

3. Today was gonna be the day, but they'll never throw it back to you.
   By now you should've somehow realized what you're not to do.
   I don't believe that anybody feels the way I do about you now.

The Best Collections for Ukulele

The Best Songs Ever

70 songs have now been arranged for ukulele. Includes: Always • Bohemian Rhapsody • Memory • My Favorite Things • Over the Rainbow • Piano Man • What a Wonderful World • Yesterday • You Raise Me Up • and more.

00282413 . . . . $17.99

Campfire Songs for Ukulele

30 favorites to sing as you roast marshmallows and strum your uke around the campfire. Includes: God Bless the U.S.A. • Hallelujah • The House of the Rising Sun • I Walk the Line • Puff the Magic Dragon • Wagon Wheel • You Are My Sunshine • and more.

00129170 . . . . $14.99

The Daily Ukulele

arr. Liz and Jim Beloff
Strum a different song everyday with easy arrangements of 365 of your favorite songs in one big songbook! Includes favorites by the Beatles, Beach Boys, and Bob Dylan, folk songs, pop songs, kids' songs, Christmas carols, and Broadway and Hollywood tunes, all with a spiral binding for ease of use.

00240356 Original Edition $39.99
00240681 Leap Year Edition $39.99
00119270 Portable Edition $37.50

Disney Hits for Ukulele

Play 23 of your favorite Disney songs on your ukulele. Includes: The Bare Necessities • Cruella De Vil • Do You Want to Build a Snowman? • Kiss the Girl • Lava • Let It Go • Once upon a Dream • A Whole New World • and more.

00151250 . . . . $16.99

Also available:

00291547 **Disney Fun Songs for Ukulele** . . . $16.99
00701708 **Disney Songs for Ukulele** $14.99
00334696 **First 50 Disney Songs on Ukulele** . $16.99

First 50 Songs You Should Play on Ukulele

An amazing collec-tion of 50 accessible, must-know favorites: Edelweiss • Hey, Soul Sister • I Walk the Line • I'm Yours • Imagine • Over the Rainbow • Peaceful Easy Feeling • The Rainbow Connection • Riptide • more.

00149250 . . . . $16.99

Also available:

00292082 **First 50 Melodies on Ukulele** . . . $15.99
00289029 **First 50 Songs on Solo Ukulele** . . $15.99
00347437 **First 50 Songs to Strum on Uke** . $16.99

40 Most Streamed Songs for Ukulele

40 top hits that sound great on uke! Includes: Despacito • Feel It Still • Girls like You • Happier • Havana • High Hopes • The Middle • Perfect • 7 Rings • Shallow • Shape of You • Something Just like This • Stay • Sucker • Sunflower • Sweet but Psycho • Thank U, Next • There's Nothing Holdin' Me Back • Without Me • and more!

00298113 . . . . $17.99

The 4 Chord Songbook

With just 4 chords, you can play 50 hot songs on your ukulele! Songs include: Brown Eyed Girl • Do Wah Diddy Diddy • Hey Ya! • Ho Hey • Jessie's Girl • Let It Be • One Love • Stand by Me • Toes • With or Without You • and many more.

00142050 . . . . $16.99

Also available:

00141143 **The 3-Chord Songbook** $16.99

Pop Songs for Kids

30 easy pop favorites for kids to play on uke, including: Brave • Can't Stop the Feeling! • Feel It Still • Fight Song • Happy • Havana • House of Gold • How Far I'll Go • Let It Go • Remember Me (Ernesto de la Cruz) • Rewrite the Stars • Roar • Shake It Off • Story of My Life • What Makes You Beautiful • and more.

00284415 . . . . $16.99

Simple Songs for Ukulele

50 favorites for standard G-C-E-A ukulele tuning, including: All Along the Watchtower • Can't Help Falling in Love • Don't Worry, Be Happy • Ho Hey • I'm Yours • King of the Road • Sweet Home Alabama • You Are My Sunshine • and more.

00156815 . . . . $14.99

Also available:

00276644 **More Simple Songs for Ukulele** . $14.99

Top Hits of 2020

18 uke-friendly tunes of 2020 are featured in this collection of melody, lyric and chord arrangements in standard G-C-E-A tuning. Includes: Adore You (Harry Styles) • Before You Go (Lewis Capaldi) • Cardigan (Taylor Swift) • Daisies (Katy Perry) • I Dare You (Kelly Clarkson) • Level of Concern (twenty one pilots) • No Time to Die (Billie Eilish) • Rain on Me (Lady Gaga feat. Ariana Grande) • Say So (Doja Cat) • and more.

00355553 . . . . $14.99

Also available:

00302274 **Top Hits of 2019** $14.99

Ukulele: The Most Requested Songs

Strum & Sing Series
Cherry Lane Music
Nearly 50 favorites all expertly arranged for ukulele! Includes: Bubbly • Build Me Up, Buttercup • Cecilia • Georgia on My Mind • Kokomo • L-O-V-E • Your Body Is a Wonderland • and more.

02501453 . . . . $14.99

The Ultimate Ukulele Fake Book

Uke enthusiasts will love this giant, spiral-bound collection of over 400 songs for uke! Includes: Crazy • Dancing Queen • Downtown • Fields of Gold • Happy • Hey Jude • 7 Years • Summertime • Thinking Out Loud • Thriller • Wagon Wheel • and more.

00175500 9" x 12" Edition $45.00
00319997 5.5" x 8.5" Edition $39.99

Order today from your favorite music retailer at
halleonard.com

Prices, contents and availability subject to change without notice

Disney characters and artwork TM & © 2021 Disney

0621
479